MEDITE DIET FOR BEGINNERS 2020

ALL YOU NEED TO KNOW ABOUT THE MEDITERRANEAN DIET TO START LOSING WEIGHT AND IMPROVE YOUR HEALTH. RESET YOUR BODY THROUGH SIMPLE AND DELICIOUS RECIPES!

By Marla Smith

TABLE OF CONTENTS

INTRODUCTION 2

CHAPTER 1.   WHAT IS THE MEDITERRANEAN DIET? 3

CHAPTER 2.   THE HISTORY OF THE MEDITERRANEAN DIET 14

CHAPTER 3.   THE SCIENCE BEHIND THE MEDITERRANEAN DIET 17

CHAPTER 4.   THE MEDITERRANEAN LIFESTYLE 20

CHAPTER 5.   HEALTH BENEFITS OF THE MEDITERRANEAN DIET 22

CHAPTER 6.   STEP BY STEP INSTRUCTIONS TO ROLL OUT THE IMPROVEMENT 30

CHAPTER 7.   A DELICIOUS PATH TO WEIGHT LOSS 33

CHAPTER 8.   ESSENTIAL MEDITERRANEAN FOOD 40

CHAPTER 9.   PLANNING YOUR MEDITERRANEAN DIET 47

CHAPTER 10. 21-DAY MEAL PLAN 51

CHAPTER 11. BREAKFAST & BRUNCH RECIPES 55

CHAPTER 12. LUNCH RECIPES 90

CHAPTER 13. DINNER RECIPES 124

CHAPTER 14. SNACKS RECIPES 159

CHAPTER 15. DESSERT RECIPES 188

CONCLUSION 214

Introduction

In this book, you'll learn everything you need to get started on the Mediterranean diet. The Mediterranean diet is all about living well and eating like the people of the Mediterranean. This includes vegetables, grains, legumes, dairy, eggs, poultry and smaller amounts of red meat. It's about dining with friends, moderate physical activity, and food that will lift your spirits. It's all about eating the traditional food of the countries that make up the Mediterranean, including Italy, Spain, France, Greece, Israel, and even Turkey. This diet promotes overall health, including weight loss, and it's great at helping reduce the risk of Parkinson's, Alzheimer's, promoting heart health, and reducing the risk of cancer.

With the Mediterranean Diet you'll have foods that are based on vegetable, fruits, grains, olive oil, nuts, beans, legumes, herbs, spices and seeds. You'll consume fish and seafood often, with cheese, yogurt and other dairy products in moderation. Poultry and eggs are allowed in moderation, but you shouldn't eat them more than twice a week. Other meats and sweets should be eaten rarely, and drinking water is encouraged. Say goodbye to sodas, and replace it with a glass of red wine in the evenings and water to hydrate. While physical activity isn't required on this diet, at least moderate activity is encouraged if you to get the most out of the Mediterranean lifestyle. Even taking an evening stroll can help to elevate the effects of the diet, including weight loss.

Chapter 1. What is the Mediterranean diet?

The Mediterranean diet refers to the traditional eating habits and lifestyles of people living around the Mediterranean Sea – Italy, Spain, France, Greece, and some North African countries. The Mediterranean diet has become very popular in recent times, as people from these regions have better health and suffer from fewer ailments, such as cancer and cardiovascular issues. Food plays a key role in this.

Research has uncovered the many benefits of this diet. According to the results of a 2013 study, many overweight and diabetic patients showed a surprising improvement in their cardiovascular health after eating the Mediterranean diet for 5 years. The study was conducted among 7000 people in Spain. There was a marked 30% reduction in cardiovascular disease in this high-risk group.

The report took the world by storm after the New England Journal of Medicine published the findings. Several studies have indicated its many health benefits – the Mediterranean diet may stabilize the level of blood sugar, prevent Alzheimer's disease, reduce the risk of heart disease and stroke, improve brain health, ease anxiety and depression, promote weight loss, and even lower the risk of certain types of cancer.

The diet differs from country to country, and even within the regions of these countries because of cultural, ethnic, agricultural, religious, and economic differences. So there is no one standard Mediterranean diet. However, there are several common factors.

The Mediterranean Diet Pyramid

The Med diet food pyramid is a nutrition guide to help people eat the right foods in the correct quantities and the prescribed frequency as per the traditional eating habits of people from the Mediterranean coast countries.

The pyramid was developed by the World Health Organization, Harvard School of Public Health, and the old ways Preservation Trust in 1993.

There are 6 food layers in the pyramid with physical activity at the base, which is an important element to maintain a healthy life.

Just above it is the first food layer, consisting of whole grains, breads, beans, pasta, and nuts. It is the strongest layer having foods that are recommended by the Mediterranean diet. Next comes fruits and vegetables. As you move up the pyramid, you will find foods that must be eaten less and less, with the topmost layer consisting of foods that should be avoided or restricted.

The Mediterranean diet food pyramid is easy to understand. It provides an easy way to follow the eating plan.

The Food Layers
1. Whole Grains, Breads, Beans – The lowest and the widest layer with foods that are strongly recommended. Your meals should be made of mostly these items. Eat whole-wheat bread, whole-wheat pita, whole-grain roll and bun,

whole-grain cereal, whole-wheat pasta, and brown rice. 4 t0 6 servings a day will give you plenty of nutrition.

2. Fruits, Vegetables – Almost as important as the lowest layer. Eat non-starchy vegetables daily like asparagus, broccoli, beets, tomatoes, carrots, cucumber, cabbage, cauliflower, turnips 4 to 8 servings daily. Take 2 to 4 servings of fruits every day. Choose seasonal fresh fruits.

3. Olive oil – Cook your meals preferably in extra-virgin olive oil. Daily consumption. Healthy for the body, it lowers the low-density lipoprotein cholesterol (LDL) and total cholesterol level. Up to 2 tablespoons of olive oil is allowed. The diet also allows canola oil.

4. Fish – Now we come to the food layers that have to be consumed weekly and not daily. You can have fish 2 to 3 times a week. Best is fatty sea fish like tuna, herring, salmon, and sardines. Sea fish will give you heart-healthy omega-3 fatty acids and plenty of proteins. Shellfish, including mussels, oysters, shrimp, and clams are also good.

5. Poultry, cheese, yogurt – The diet should include cheese, yogurt, eggs, chicken, and other poultry products, but in moderation. Maximum 2-3 times in a week. Low-fat dairy is best. Soy milk, cheese, or yogurt is better.

6. Meats, sweets – This is the topmost layer consisting of foods that are best avoided. You can have them once or twice in a month max. Remember, the Mediterranean diet is plant-based. There is very little room for meat, especially

red meat. If you cannot live without it, then take red meat in small portions. Choose lean cuts. Have sweets only to celebrate. For instance, you can have a couple of sweets after following the diet for a month.

Recommended Foods

For example, most people living in the region eat a diet rich in whole grains, vegetables, fruits, nuts, seeds, fish, fats, and legumes. It is not a restrictive diet like the many low-fat eating plans. Actually, fat is encouraged, but only from healthy sources, such as polyunsaturated fat (omega-3 fatty acids) that you will get from fish and monounsaturated fat from olive oil.

It is strongly plant-based, but not exclusively vegetarian. The diet recommends limiting the intake of saturated fats and trans fats that you get from red meat and processed foods. You must also limit the intake of dairy products.

- Fruits and vegetables – Eat daily. Try to have 7-10 servings every day. Meals are strongly based on plant-based foods. Eat fresh fruits and vegetables. Pick from seasonal varieties.
- Whole grains – Eat whole-grain cereal, bread, and pasta. All parts of whole grains – the germ, bran, and the endosperm provide healthy nutrients. These nutrients are lost when the grain is refined into white flour.
- Healthy fats only – Avoid butter for cooking. Switch to olive oil. Dip your bread in flavored olive oil instead of

applying margarine or butter on bread. Trans fats and saturated fats can cause heart disease.

- Fish – Fish is encouraged. Eat fatty fish like herring, mackerel, albacore tuna, sardines, lake trout, and salmon. Fatty fish will give you plenty of healthy omega-3 fatty acids that reduce inflammations. Omega-3 fatty acids also reduced blood clotting, decreased triglycerides, and improves heart health. Eat fresh seafood two times a week. Avoid deep-fried fish. Choose grilled fish.

- Legumes – Provides the body with minerals, protein, complex carbohydrates, polyunsaturated fatty acids, and fiber. Eat daily.

- Dairy and poultry – You can eat eggs, milk products, and chicken throughout the week, but with moderation. Restrict cheese. Go for plain or low-fat Greek yogurt instead of cheese.

- Nuts and seeds – 3 or more servings every week. Eat a variety of nuts, seeds, and beans. Walnuts and almonds are all allowed.

- Red meat – The Mediterranean diet is not meat-based. You can still have red meat, but only once or twice a week max. If you love red meat, then make sure that it is lean. Take small portions only. Avoid processed meats like salami, sausage, and bologna.

- Olive Oil – The key source of fat. Olive oil will give you monounsaturated fat that lowers the LDL or low-density lipoprotein cholesterol and total cholesterol level. Seeds and nuts will also provide you monounsaturated fat. You can also have canola oil but no cream, butter, mayonnaise, or margarine. Take up to 4 tablespoons of olive oil a day. For best results, only take extra-virgin olive oil.
- Wine – Red wine is allowed, but with moderation. Don't take more than a glass of red wine daily. Best take only 3-4 days a week.
- Desserts – Say no to ice cream, sweets, pies, and chocolate cake. Fresh fruits are good.

Main Components –

- Focus on natural foods – Avoid processed foods as much as you can
- Be flexible – Plan to have a variety of foods
- Consume fruits, vegetables, healthy fats, and whole grains daily
- Have weekly plans for poultry, fish, eggs, and beans
- Take dairy products moderately
- Limit red meat intake
- Take water instead of soda. Only take wine when you are having a meal.

Foods in the Traditional Mediterranean Diet

Whole Grains	Vegetables	Fruits	Protein	Dairy	Others
Brown rice	Artichokes	Apples	Almonds	Low/non-fat plain or Greek yogurt	Bay leaf
Oats	Arugula	Apricots	Walnuts	Manchego cheese	Basil
Bulgur	Beats	Avocados	Pistachios	Brie cheese	Olive oil
Barley	Broccoli	Figs	Cannellini Beans	Ricotta cheese	Red wine
Farrow	Cucumbers	Olives	Chickpeas	Parmesan cheese	Mint

Wheat berries	Eggplant	Strawberries	Kidney beans	Feta cheese	Pepper
Pasta	Onions	Tomatoes	Salmon		cumin
Whole grain bread	Spinach	Melons	Tuna		Garlic
Couscous	Potatoes	Grapes	Eggs		Anise spice

Foods Allowed

You should consume plenty of fruits, vegetables, nuts, seeds, beans, whole grains, herbs, and legumes. Olive oil and canola oil are both allowed.

Eat Moderately

Fish, seafood, chicken, eggs, low-fat cheese, and yogurt.

Restricted Foods

This list includes refined grains like white rice, white bread, sweets, baked products, and soda. Also, restrict processed meats and red meat.

Watch out for high-fat dairy products like butter and ice cream and trans-fats in margarine and processed foods.

Med Diet Serving Sizes

Food Groups and Daily/Weekly Servings	Serving Sizes
Non-starchy vegetables – 4 to 8 servings	1 serving is ½ cup of cooked vegetables or 1 cup of raw vegetables Asparagus, artichoke, broccoli, beets, Brussels sprouts, cabbage, celery, cauliflower, carrots, eggplant, tomatoes, cucumber, onion, zucchini, turnips, mushrooms, and salad greens and. Note: Peas, corn, and potatoes are starchy vegetables.
Fruits – 2 to 4 servings	One serving is a small fruit or ½ cup juice or ¼ cup dried fruit Eat fresh fruits for their nutrients and fiber. You can also have canned fruits with their juice and frozen fruits without added sugar.
Legumes, Nuts, Seeds – 2 to 4 servings	Legumes – 1 serving is ½ cup cooked kidney, pinto, garbanzo, soy, navy beans, lentils, or split peas, or ¼ cup fat-free beans. Nuts and Seeds – 1 serving is 2 tablespoons of sesame or sunflower seeds, 1 tablespoon peanut butter, 7-8 pecans or walnuts, 12-15 almonds, 20

	peanuts. Take 1-2 servings of nuts or seeds and 1-2 servings of legumes. Legumes will give you minerals, fiber, and protein, whole nuts provide unsaturated fat without increasing your LDL cholesterol levels.
Low-Fat Dairy – 2 to 3 servings	1 serving is 1 cup of skim milk, non-fat yogurt, or 1 oz. low-fat cheese Replace dairy products with soy yogurt, calcium-rich soy milk, or soy cheese. You need a vitamin D and calcium supplement if you are taking less than 2 servings daily.
Fish – 2 to 3 times a week	One serving is 3 ounces Bake, sauté, roast, broil, poach, or grill. It is best to eat fatty fish, such as sardines, herring, salmon, or mackerel. Fish will provide you omega-3 fats, which offers many health benefits.
Poultry – 1 to 3 times a week	One serving is 3 ounces Sauté, bake, grill, or stir fry the poultry. Eat without the skin.
Whole grains, starchy vegetables – 4 to 6 servings	One serving is 1 ounce of – ½ cup sweet potatoes, potatoes, corn, or peas 1 slice of whole-wheat bread 1 small whole-grain roll ½ large whole-grain bun 6 whole-grain crackers

	6-inch whole wheat pita ½ cup cooked brown rice, whole-wheat pasta, or barley ½ cup whole-grain cereal (cracked wheat, oatmeal, quinoa) Whole grains provide fiber and keep the stomach full, promoting weight loss.
Healthy fats – 4 to 6 servings	One serving is – 1 tablespoon of regular salad dressing 2 tablespoons of light salad dressing 2 teaspoons light margarine 1 teaspoon canola or olive oil 1 teaspoon regular mayonnaise 1/8 avocado 5 olives These are mostly unsaturated fats, so your LDL cholesterol levels won't increase.
Alcohol	Men – Max 2 drinks a day. Women – Max 1 drink a day. 1 drink = 4 ounces of wine, 12-ounce beer, or 1-1/2-ounces liquor (vodka, whiskey, brandy, etc.). Avoid alcohol if you have high triglycerides or high BP.

Chapter 2. The History of the Mediterranean diet

Just like it sounds, the Mediterranean diet comes from the dietary traditions of the people of the Mediterranean isle region such as the Romans and Greeks. The people of these regions had a rich diet full of fruits, bread, wine, olive oil, nuts, and seafood. Despite the fatty elements in their diet, the people of this region tended to live longer and overall healthy lives with relatively less cardiovascular heart issues. This phenomenon was noticed by American scientist Ancel Keys in the 1950s.

Keys was an academic researcher at the University of Minnesota in the 1950s who researched healthy eating habits and how to reverse the decline in American cardiovascular health. He found in his research that poor people in the Mediterranean region of the world were healthier compared to the rich American population which had seen a recent rise in cardiovascular heart issues and obesity. Compared to wealthy New Yorkers, the lower class in the Mediterranean lived well into their 90s and tended to be physically active in their senior years. Keys and his team of scientists decided to travel the world and study the link between the region's diet and the health of the people who lived there. In 1957, he traveled and studied the lifestyles, nutrition, exercise, and diet of the United States, Italy, Holland, Greece, Japan, Finland, and Yugoslavia. Twenty years later, he published his findings in a landmark study called "The Seven Countries Study." It evaluated the diets and lifestyles of these regions.

Keys' research found that the dietary choices of the people from the Mediterranean region allowed them to live a longer lifespan and one that kept them more physically active compared to other world populations. The people of Greece, in particular, ate a diet that consisted of healthy fats like seafood, nuts, olive oil, and fatty fish. Despite the amount of fat in these sources, their cardiovascular health stayed consistent without the risk factors for a heart attack or stroke. His study became a guideline for the United States to set its own nutritional standards, and he became known as the father of nutritional science.

With Keys' work leading the way, further research and clinical trials have been conducted on the Mediterranean diet which gives evidence for its health-improving properties. Not only will you lose weight, but you could lower your LDL "bad" cholesterol, lower your blood pressure, and decrease and stabilize blood sugar levels. With a decrease in these signs of cardiovascular heart disease, you can greatly reduce your risk of suffering from heart attack, stroke, or premature death.

It's important to point out that the Mediterranean diet cannot alone bring about these changes to someone's health. It will depend on a variety of other factors in their lifestyle such as genetics, physical exercise, smoking, obesity, drug use, etc. Part of the combination of the Mediterranean diet is incorporating physical exercise into your life. That's how it goes from the Mediterranean "diet" to a Mediterranean "lifestyle" that truly mimics the people of that region. The people of Greece tend to live an active lifestyle with some sort of daily physical activity they partake in. Whether that is walking, sailing, rowing, swimming, or hiking, coupling that physical exercise that with a healthy plant-based diet is what can bring about the beneficial health results. In our current environment, physical activity could mean a session at the gym or even just a walk around the block. It doesn't have to highly intensive, but the important part is incorporating some sort of physical activity in your day, so you can truly gain the benefits of following this diet.

Before we begin listing a rudimentary list of what you can and cannot eat, it's important to highlight that the Mediterranean region consists of many countries with their own unique dietary choices. With this diversity comes many varieties of recipes that you can incorporate into your dishes as long as you are still following the healthy tenets of the Mediterranean diet. This gives a basic outline of which foods you should include on your shopping list and then you can look for recipes from there! What does the basic Mediterranean diet look like?

- Your diet should consist heavily of whole grain bread, extra virgin olive oil, fresh fruits and vegetables, herbs and spices, nuts and seeds, fish and seafood

- You should moderately eat: poultry, cheese, egg, yogurt

- You should try to rarely eat: red meat and organ meat

- You should avoid the following: processed snacks, refined oils (canola oil or vegetable oil), refined grains (white bread), sugary drinks (juice, soda), processed meats (hot dogs, sausages, bacon), trans fats

- You should drink: water, wine

Chapter 3. The Science Behind the Mediterranean Diet

Most of the benefits of this form of diet come from a large number of plant foods associated with the diet. By incorporating a large number of fresh fruits and fresh vegetables in your diet, you are getting a high number of antioxidants and free radicals which are helpful for your body's cellular system and metabolism. The high intake of vitamins, minerals, and fiber you're getting from these plant sources can lower your risk of diabetes, constipation and bowel issues, and heart disease.

Since we've mentioned the Mediterranean diet's intake of healthy fats, it's important to go over why these are healthier for the body. Most of the fat is monounsaturated such as the fat you get from olive oil. This fat, found in nuts, seeds, and oil, tends to be healthier for the body compared to the saturated fat that is found in meat and poultry. A high amount of saturated fat is what tends to wreak havoc on the body's cholesterol and blood pressure.

By staying low in red meat intake, the Mediterranean diet harnesses protein sources from fish and seafood which are healthier for the body. They are high in omega 3 fatty acids. The research regarding omega 3 fatty acids is recent, covering the last 20 to 30 years, but it's shown to be an essential element for vision and brain health, as well as fetal health if a woman is pregnant. Adults are advised to consume at least 250 to 500 milligrams of fatty acids a day. Since most of us don't eat fish every day, you can get in the form of a fish oil supplement. With the Mediterranean diet, that won't be as necessary. The people of the

Mediterranean had easy access to fishing and considered fresh fish and seafood a staple in their diet. Not only are there so many varieties, but it also is much healthier for you than having red meat many times a week which tends to raise your cholesterol and clog your arteries. You can still have red meat on this diet, but you should try to consume it more rarely and be aware of your portion sizes. And if you do have red meat, you want to ensure that you are also having healthy vegetables or whole grains along with it.

Along with food, it's important to note that drinking alcohol in moderation is a big part of the Mediterranean diet. Recent studies in the last decade have shown that moderate consumption of red wine could considerably lessen the risk of heart related diseases, gallstones, and diabetes (Type 2). It's believed that red wine contains a component called resveratrol which has health benefits in animals and humans. With this consumption, it's important to note that it is to be moderate, about a glass a day for women, and 2 for men. But with it can come health dangers for pregnant women or birth defects in babies. Many declare alcohol consumption as optional in the diet because some people may be restricted due to health or religious reasons.

We can't speak about the science behind the Mediterranean diet without speaking in length about extra virgin olive oil. With the abundance of olives in the Mediterranean region, olive oil is essential for all their cooking needs. That includes baking, seasoning, frying, and as a fat element in salad vinaigrettes. But when it comes to olive oil, the best oil will be labeled as "extra virgin" because it is the most unprocessed version of olive oil, so the purest that is available. There are many components in extra virgin olive oil that make it such a healthy substance. It contains a high amount of vitamin E which has anti-inflammatory properties for the body. It also has a high amount of phenol substances which contains similar health properties. Oleic acid is another property that is healthy for the heart. It's present in significant amounts in olive oil as compared to other oil types. When it comes to the properties of olive oil, it's taken very seriously by the culinary community. There's an International Olive Council that tests the levels of phenol and acidity in different brands of olive oil to ensure they qualify for the label of "extra virgin". The rule when it comes to olive oil is to go with the old saying "quality over quantity." Most nutritionists will say that consuming 4 to 5 tbsp of olive oil a day should be enough for all your cooking needs. That includes salad dressings, pan frying, baking, or seasoning your food. Olive oil should be kept away from direct sunlight and heat to avoid degradation of the oil.

When we see all these qualities of the Mediterranean diet and how they play out for the body, it's easy to see how this diet can help you improve your health. By including exercise in your routine, you are also gaining the possibility of better health and strengthening your heart and losing more weight. Along with the health benefits possible, the ease of the Mediterranean diet appeals to many people. No counting calories, no measuring food portions, or keeping track of your daily macronutrients. With this flexibility and simply knowing the right foods to eat and avoid, the Mediterranean can be a very easy lifestyle to follow if you are hoping to improve your health.

Chapter 4.   The Mediterranean Lifestyle

Not just the food, but the correct lifestyle is also equally important. This includes both getting adequate exercise and making social connections.

Physical Activity – It is at the base of the food pyramid, even lower than the first and most important food layer – getting adequate physical activity is essential. This includes exercising regularly, swimming, biking, running, and playing an active sport. However, there are other ways as well to maintain good health.

You will find many from the Mediterranean region not going to the gym. But, they are not inactive. Many are into a lot of manual labor. They will walk to their workplace, to the bakery, or the farmer's market. They walk to their friend's home. Even a daily walk and moderate exercise will help. Natural movements are good. Avoid the escalator. Take the stairs instead.

How much exercising is good? Working out is always good for health. You don't have to lift weights, though. 10-15 minutes on the treadmill and gym bike 5 days a week should be good. Half an hour of moderate-intensity activity will do. Nothing better if you can also do a few muscle-strengthening activities twice a week. You can also try walking 200 minutes a week or even gardening for an hour 4-5 times a week.

Cook at Home – Home cooked food is always healthier than eating out. For example, restaurant cooked pasta will have higher portions of sodium. Again, you can have one portion of whole-grain spaghetti with tomato sauce and spinach instead of the heavy cream sauce. You can control the ingredients by preparing the meals at home. Home cooked meals have lots of minerals, vitamins, and fiber, and are lower in added sugar, sodium, and saturated fat.

Eat Together – The mealtime should be a social experience. Eating together with friends or family is a great stress buster. It will boost your mood, which will have a positive impact on your physical health. Plus, it will prevent you from overeating too. You will often find the Mediterranean people eating together in a garden.

Switch the TV off and enjoy your meal. Monitor what the kids are eating. If you live alone, invite a co-worker, neighbor, or friend. You can even invite someone and prepare meals together.

Laugh Often – Have you heard of the popular saying, "Laughter is the best medicine"? This is true in the Mediterranean culture. Many are individuals with a big personality. Their conversations are full of humor. They love to tell stories. Enjoy life and keep a positive attitude/

Live a Simple Life – Consider food, for example. You won't find them buying too much of anything. The idea of buying any ingredient in bulk is foreign to them. They buy fresh, focusing on daily needs. And of course, fresh food is always best.

Enjoy Every Bite – Slow down and enjoy each bite. Many will eat for survival. But in the Mediterranean belt, they love their food. They enjoy it. Don't eat on the go. Sit down and have a proper meal.

Chapter 5. Health Benefits of the Mediterranean Diet

The Mediterranean diet is a valid ally for the protection of everyone's health, as, based on vegetables, cereals, and extra virgin olive oil, it is able to bring to the body all those who are the fundamental substances for its proper operation. In this section of the book, we will share how it works and benefits to man.

How the Mediterranean diet works

The Mediterranean diet acts at various levels.

It reduces arterial hypertension, reduces bad LDL cholesterol, and increases good HDL cholesterol. It prevents and cures overweight and obesity. It helps prevent or better control type 2 diabetes.

It represents a factor that protects or stops the progression of atherosclerosis.

These benefits can be considered a real medicine both in those who only have these risk factors and in those who have already developed a heart attack.

Several components of the diet appear to have important beneficial effects.

The fish, especially the blue one, is rich in omega-3 and polyunsaturated fatty acids, which slow down the formation of atherosclerotic plaque, the first step for heart attack.

The extra-virgin olive oil, walnuts, and almonds give a good supply of the fundamental substances for the correct functioning of the body (carbohydrates, proteins, and fats) and are rich in micronutrients that have anti-atherosclerosis activity. They also reduce other risk factors for heart attack, such as high blood pressure. They improve insulin sensitivity, reducing the risk of type 2 diabetes.

The red wine is known that moderate amounts of wine promote good heart function as it is rich in resveratrol, a substance with important antioxidant activity.

Vitamin deficiency

One of the most important characteristics of the Mediterranean diet seems to be a correct balance between macro and micronutrients. Among the micronutrients, vitamins are essential for the body's well-being. The Mediterranean diet guarantees an adequate intake of both hydro and fat-soluble vitamins with great benefits.

The Mediterranean diet is rich in many important vitamins.

- A: they are the precursors of retinol, an essential vitamin for the eyesight, the glands, and the immune system. The Mediterranean diet guarantees adequate income in more than 90% of the population because it is rich in vegetables and fish.

- B: the B vitamins are water-soluble and intervene in cellular metabolism. They are abundant in cereals and white meats, essential components of the Mediterranean diet.

- C: important for repairing vessels and has an antioxidant effect. The Mediterranean diet guarantees an adequate intake of this vitamin, being rich in fruit (in particular citrus fruits) and vegetables (in particular tomatoes).

- D: Adequate intake is essential for bone health. The Mediterranean diet, abundant in fish, guarantees an optimal supply of this vitamin.

- E: has antioxidant and anti-aging properties. It is abundantly contained in wheat, corn, rice, and green legumes.

- K: has an antihemorrhagic and osteoporosis action. It is contained in abundance in green legumes, in particular, the cruciferous (broccoli, cabbage).

- Folic acid: essential for the prevention of anemias, and in cellular metabolism, they are contained in large quantities in vegetables, in particular in broad-leaved ones.

Cardiovascular disease and risk factors

Numerous studies have highlighted the important benefits of the Mediterranean diet on cardiovascular diseases. Not only on the main risk factors for these pathologies but also on the course of the disease once it occurs.

Oxidative stress and free radicals

Furthermore, all the components of the Mediterranean diet have high quantities of polyphenols, antioxidant substances, which counteract the action of free radicals and oxidative stress.

It involves the intake of high quantities of fruit and vegetables, rich in fiber. That limits the intestinal absorption of fats and slowdown that of sugars, thus preventing glycemic peaks.

Limit your intake of foods high in saturated fat such as red meats, cheeses, and sausages. Responsible, if in excess, for high cholesterol levels and, therefore, atherosclerotic risk.

Use aromatic herbs, which allow you to reduce your salt intake, thus helping to regulate blood pressure.

It is moderately low in calories, rich in fibers that increase the sense of satiety, and modulate the absorption of the various nutrients, favoring the control of body weight.

The metabolic syndrome

The set of risk factors mentioned above occurs in metabolic syndrome.

The Mediterranean diet is an important ally against this condition. Which exposes a subject to high cardiovascular risk.

Second type diabetes

A study presented by researchers reveals a new mechanism by which the Mediterranean diet could protect the vessels of people with type 2 diabetes.

The research was conducted on 215 subjects with newly diagnosed type 2 diabetes. These patients were divided into two groups. The first group was recommended a Mediterranean-type diet, the second group a non-Mediterranean low-fat diet.

At the end of the study, subjects who had followed the Mediterranean diet had significantly more endothelial progenitor cells than the other group.

Endothelial progenitor cells are young endothelial cells. That is, of the inside of the blood vessels. These cells have the function of repairing blood vessels when they are affected by ischemic damage.

It is the first diet-based study to demonstrate a beneficial effect of the Mediterranean diet on the regenerative capacity of the endothelium in a population of patients with newly diagnosed type 2 diabetes.

The study shows for the first time that following a Mediterranean diet is associated with the increase in circulating levels of endothelial cell progenitors.

These were important results, especially for patients with newly diagnosed type 2 diabetes, who were first advised to change their lifestyle with diet and structured physical activity, even before starting medical therapy.

Beneficial effects on tumors

Numerous studies have shown that the Mediterranean diet is able to reduce the risk of getting cancer.

A Mediterranean-type diet could prevent about:

- 25% of colorectal cancers
- 15-20% of breast cancers
- 10-15% of carcinomas of the prostate, endometrium, and pancreas

In fact, the Mediterranean diet has a high content of unsaturated fats, fibers, vitamins, and polyphenols, with an anti-free radical, anti-inflammatory, and antioxidant action.

Legumes contain phytoestrogens that modulate the action of sex hormones, hindering the growth of some of the most common tumors in the elderly population.

Fresh fruits and vegetables: rich in antioxidants capable of neutralizing free radicals, responsible for cellular degeneration. Vegetable fibers also regulate and improve intestinal function, freeing the body of toxins.

The fish, in particular, the blue one, is rich in omega-3 polyunsaturated fatty acids, coenzyme Q10, and selenium, antioxidant substances capable of counteracting the proliferation of cancer cells.

Extra virgin olive oil is rich in monounsaturated fatty acids, polyphenols, and vitamin E, which protect cell membranes from oxidative damage caused by free radicals.

Mediterranean diet allied to the brain

The Mediterranean diet is also the best food style to preserve our brain's decay.

In January 2017, a study from the University of Edinburgh published in the journal Neurology focused on brain size. The elderly who constantly follow this type of diet would have a less "consumed" brain than those who follow a different diet.

We know that as we age, the brain progressively loses neurons, the brain cells. This means reduced cognitive functions such as memory, learning ability, reasoning.

All the characteristics of the Mediterranean diet described above prevent the development of mild cognitive impairment and, therefore, of actual dementia.

Longevity and quality of life

An Italian study has recently shown that the Mediterranean diet improves the lifestyle of the elderly. The research was conducted by the Cnr Institute of Neuroscience and the University of Padua and published in the American Journal of Clinical Nutrition.

He highlighted how the Mediterranean diet ensures a lower prevalence of disability, depression, and pain in old age.

To reach this conclusion, the experts took into consideration 4,470 Americans with an average age of 61 years. Those who followed the Mediterranean diet have shown to have a higher quality of life, in particular, "a lower prevalence of disability and depression (about 30% less).

A diet that ensures longevity but also an excellent quality of life gained.

Chapter 6. Step by Step Instructions to Roll Out the Improvement

We are all involved in being lean, losing weight, getting a good diet plan, getting rid of cardiovascular and health-related illnesses. Typically, once you have a good diet plan such as the Mediterranean diet pan, the chances are that you will eventually reduce the number of calories in your body resulting in decreased heart-related issues.

The other benefits include weight shedding, fat burning and gradually slimming down. It is truly easy to implement diet plans like the Mediterranean diet plan. That's because you can't eat the gunk and bland vegetables that many people have to submit to just because they want to live longer and healthier.

You will enjoy delicious meals with the Mediterranean diet plan while still rising the chances of getting heart-related problems. Here are a few tips to help adopt the Mediterranean diet.

1. Decide on What Diet Type

Most of the people tend to worry about their diet plans consistently. They worry if it will work if they lose weight if they can reduce their chances of dying younger as a result of heart disease and cancer and, most importantly, worry if they can keep up with their diets. Okay, the thing is, if you really want to do this, you have to choose which choice you think works best for you.

There are two main dietary forms or regimens. You can do the form planned or the style Do-It-Yourself. It all depends on the makeup you have. For instance, some people don't like strict time tables and are more likely to fail to use them because they are instinctively opposed to things that make them feel like they're boxed in.

Though, other people find it exciting to chart a strategy and are more likely to stick to it. It all depends on the person that you are. So, whatever happens, just pick one out. If you don't know which group you're moving for, just go for one. You can always turn to the other, if you don't like it.

2. Find Recipes that Will Work for You

The taste of the people in the food is different. You need to find and stick to that which works for you. The basic components of the Mediterranean diet plan include, among others, olive oil, legumes, vegetables, nuts, grains, unprocessed carbohydrates, fish, reduced red meat consumption and saturated fat.

Now, if you just like eating them like that, then it's all right. But if you want to make it much more fun, you'd have to find recipes that work. The South Beach Diet recipes, for example, are great and fun to cook. So, find recipes that inculcate these and which are based on the Mediterranean diet.

3. Get Creative With the Diet

Since following a few diet plans, the reason many people return to eating junk is that the diets are either dull, repetitive or lacking in flavor. So, what you should do is just go for those delicious meals. Get yourself creative with the recipes. Try something new, and something different. Chances are if you're looking well enough, you'll find lots of Mediterranean diet recipes that will last you for a whole year and more.

4. Be Disciplined

Because the Mediterranean diet is really simple to use and apply, it is hardly called a diet by some. I just see it as an alternative lifestyle and food choices that help you stay healthy and live longer. The secret, then, is discipline. Stay focused and who knows, you could just give yourself an extra 15 years of health and life.

Chapter 7.   A Delicious Path to Weight Loss

If you have attempted a lot of diets in the past, you will realize it can be a challenge finding a diet that is multi-faceted. This means that looking for a diet that will achieve weight loss, as well as keep you in optimum health, is difficult. Through this book so far, you have been able to learn a lot more about the Mediterranean diet, and you will realize it serves more than just one purpose. This makes it fairly obvious why many people from across the globe are now adopting the diet.

Some of the most outstanding reasons it is to become people's favorite diet plan include the fact it has been shown to improve the quality of life in terms of health status. In the countries where the diet originated, people seem to have a longer lifespan, and it is also a very effective diet to follow if you wish to cut down on unnecessary weight or simply correct your body figure. It is not a diet of deprivation; rather, it is a diet of moderation. It illustrates that making the right decisions, concerning what you eat, can uplift your life dramatically.

If your reason for adopting the Mediterranean diet is to get more insight on how you can shed weight and learn to stick to a regime that works, make sure you pay special attention to this section. Weight loss and one's outlook are matters that are dear to many people, and that is why people need to continue to learn that the Mediterranean diet plan is not a quick-fix to weight issue, neither is it a tedious, mundane regime that you have to bore yourself to death with. It is about considering a change in your lifestyle that will increase your happiness in leaps and bounds, especially how you feel about your physical body. Here are a few guidelines, which if properly adhered, will make the journey to adopting the Mediterranean diet fun and worthwhile.

The Mediterranean Diet is a series of health choices

It simply means you have to constantly and consciously choose good foods over the bad ones that are otherwise referred to as fast food and rich man's foods, like the burgers and other highly processed chemically-made foods. Although many people may argue they may not be aware that certain foods are unhealthy, they do not make a valid argument. You need to take a commonsensical approach to your food. Is it in its natural form? How has it been prepared? Does it contain a significant amount of added sugar? Have others labelled it as unhealthy? It is time to make the right choices.

The most important task for you as you make this healthy choice is to take a careful note of what the diet comprises, and each day choose to have a combination of three of the ingredients from those that make up the Mediterranean Diet that form a balanced diet. Other choices you have to make, in addition to choosing healthy foods, is the decision to control your calorie intake by managing your intake portions day by day. The easiest way to do this is to choose a smaller plate. By doing so, you will immediately begin to eat smaller portions, but you can still fill your plate the same way as if you were eating from a larger one.

Paying attention to lifestyle changes

The Mediterranean diet does not just focus on the food you eat, but also, to a large extent, how you live your life. You must have read by now about the history of the diet. Those from the Mediterranean origin, who strictly observed this diet, understood the importance of family and friends, and this is why meal times were revered in high regard. It is during these meal times that people would share their life experiences, and it was believed this sharing helped the participants deal with any stressful situation they might have been going through. What this is driving at is, the Mediterranean diet and stress do not mix. It is a diet that advocates you to have an excellent mental state, just as much as to fix yourself physically, inside and out.

One of the other areas to which you have to pay attention is the portions of food you consume. If you carefully study the diet, you will realize it entails some good proportion of carbohydrates and proteins, which, if not consumed in moderation, can have the effect of making you add weight, contrary to your expectation. The other component of the diet that you have to use in moderation is wine. It forms an integral part of the Mediterranean diet, but this does not in any way give you the leeway to overindulge in alcohol. Remember that the more wine you take, the more food you tend to eat, because wine has the effect of speeding up digestion.

Exercise is important

Even the people of old will tell you that all work with no play makes Jack a dull boy. In relation to the Mediterranean diet, if you work on getting your food portions and component right, but do not engage in physical activity to help your body assimilate the food properly, then you might as well forget about your weight loss goals. Slow down your fast-paced lifestyle and simply take the time to smell the flowers and to enjoy nature as you take a walk in the park or enjoy some swimming sessions.

Almost all diets mention the component of exercise is important, but on this diet, it is essential. You must exercise each day, whether it is light exercise or something intense that really gets your blood flowing. If possible, exercise with a loved one so you can share the experience and have just as much of an effect on your mind as you would on your body.

Set realistic goals

Do not just set the goals; stick to them. You definitely do not want to come up with goals you cannot realize and then blame it on the diet and conclude that it does not work. For example, even if you were consuming just the food components in the Mediterranean diet pyramid, but heaping your plate with excess amounts and doing no exercise, it would definitely not be the diet's fault that you added more weight instead of losing. However, if you consider taking in low-calorie foods in large quantities and more frequently, for example fruits and vegetables, you are good to go. This may seem like straightforward and logical reasoning, but when it comes to issues of body weight, many people become unreasonable and make every possible excuse they can. Eat right, exercise, and you will most assuredly, lose your excess weight.

Say no to food cravings

Do you know why people tend to find it very challenging to realize their goal of losing weight within a specified time? It is the little devil called craving. It is true that cravings could be a result of physiological or psychological factors or a combination of both, but they need to be dealt with accordingly. What do you do when you feel the urge to snack on sweet things, like chocolate? It is likely that you reach out for them and take in 'just a little bit'. Usually, what would happen is you start small, and ten minutes later, you are staring at an empty wrapper with a guilty look on your face.

Change this destructive behavior as you choose this wholesome diet. Choose to take a cup of water or yogurt instead. Other suggestions for dealing with cravings are ensuring you do not skip meals, as this only makes the craving worse. The result of this is binge eating, or eating the foods that are wrong for you in excess. You should also ensure that you eat more proteins, such as fish, a little often as this will slow down digestion a bit, hence, reducing chances of a full-blown chocolate craving. The right foods will fill you up and balance your body, so sugar and carb cravings are kept at bay.

Fruits, vegetables, and nuts, if incorporated during a meal, will keep away the urge to snack on sweet bites every now and then. They are rich in fiber and the right fats, and they contain sugar in its natural form.

Quit diets once and for all

With all the information available in the various diets you can try in order to lose weight, you are bound to get confused and especially so if you try to work on them as you observe the Mediterranean diet regime. You must have read about those diets that advise you to keep off carbohydrates and proteins and purely cut down to fruits and vegetables only.

There are also diets that insist you should live on soup and health shakes for a long period. Or even some that cut down your intake of certain food groups completely. What such diets don't point out is that you need carbohydrates to energize your body and proteins to build the body. This is the reason most of these diets do not work for long, because at some point, low energy and blood sugar level will dictate that you eat heavy foods. As long as the body receives what it requires in the right quantities, it will balance itself and lead you to a healthy weight. The moment you abuse your body by making the wrong food choices, some of which border on the extreme, the easier it becomes to fall off the wagon on fad diets.

Do away with stress

Stress is controllable; it is just a matter of how you choose to respond to stressors and factors that trigger you to become unhappy. Learn how to manage your stress factors in simple ways, like getting enough sleep, meditating, exercising, and deep breathing and walking away from stressful situations, it is possible. Practice this and watch as the Mediterranean diet transforms you into the person you want to be. Another way this diet helps you relieve the stresses you face each day is the focus on family and relationships, sharing meals, and experiences. When you have someone to share with, what could have appeared as a large issue, is brought back down to size.

Chapter 8.   Essential Mediterranean Food

The principle behind Mediterranean dishes is natural, simple ingredients that can be found on the coast region. This leads to a variety of vegetables, fruit, whole grains, beans, healthy fats, red wine, beef, and fish. It's considered one of the healthiest diets.

Fruits & Vegetables

The first part of the Mediterranean diet is fresh fruits and vegetables. Most vegetables and fruits are low in fat and high in fiber, which make them heart healthy. They can help with weight loss too.

They're also full of antioxidants which can help to reduce inflammation and slow down the aging process.

The antioxidants include vitamins A, vitamin C, vitamin E and vitamin K. they can help to remove harmful free radicals that can cause the oxidation of LDL, also known as bad cholesterol.

Whole Grains

This is also a must for the Mediterranean diet. Refined grains have been stripped of nutrients during the refinement process, which means they aren't as healthy as whole grains which have more nutrition. Whole grains have bran, endosperm and germ which are great for your health.

Some whole grain examples are brown rice, barley, bulgur, millet, oat, rye, teff, and wheat. Whole grains have quite a few benefits as well since they are more satisfying to your hunger and have phytochemicals which are disease-fighting chemicals.

Using Olive Oil

Olive oil has a lot of monounsaturated fats which can protect against heart disease because it keeps LDL levels, bad cholesterol, low and HDL levels, good cholesterol, high. Most Mediterranean meals are prepared by liberally using olive oil. Also, on the Mediterranean diet most foods are grilled or baked, which is easier to do with olive oil.

Fish & Chicken

The Mediterranean diet often includes and abundance of fresh fish because of the proximity of the area to the sea. Fish has a lot of omega-3 fatty acids which have various heart healthy benefits including reducing triglycerides, inflammation and even cholesterol. There are various types of fish to choose from as well, including salmon, mackerel, herring, sardines, trout and albacore tuna. Chicken can also be used in place of fish to replace red meat. It isn't as healthy as fish, but it does have lower saturated fats and cholesterol than red meat.

Nuts

Unsalted nuts are often eaten as a snack in Mediterranean countries. However, the US is more likely to go for things such as crackers or potato chips which have no health benefits. Nuts can also be included in desserts and savory dishes. Pine nuts can be used to make homemade pesto, and you'll find walnuts are often in bread dough. Nuts are a wonderful source of monounsaturated fat, and they're packed full of protein and fiber. They can also contain various minerals and vitamins which will help to improve your overall health.

Red Wine

Small amounts of alcohol is consumed with most meals, especially red wine, in Mediterranean countries. It's been proven that alcoholic drinks, such as red wine, have healthy heart benefits. Red wine has an antioxidant called flavonoids which can prevent fatty deposits from building up in the artery walls. Even the American Heart Association recommends one to two drinks a day for men and women. These drinks are only suppose to be four ounces each.

Spices

There are many spices and herbs that are used in the Mediterranean diet that also provide health benefits, including garlic. While these herbs and spices help to make the food taste great, their benefits to your health is the real magic.

The most common herbs and spices in this area are garlic, anise, basil, bay leaf, fennel, lavender, cumin, mint, marjoram, oregano, pepper, rosemary, sumaci, parsley, thyme and tarragon. Cutting down on salt can help to lower blood pressure, which is also a risk for heart disease, and these flavors help to lower your intake of salt. Garlic is a great way to spice up your meal, and you may not even know that the salt is missing!

Dairy

Full fat dairy products, including cheese and whole milk, are eaten in small amounts in Mediterranean countries. This helps to keep the saturated fat intake down. However, traditional cheeses such as goat cheese and feta cheese are lower in fat than hard cheeses such as Cheddar, which is extremely popular in the US. There is also yogurt which is eaten more frequently by being included in various dishes and desserts which is very healthy. Eggs can also be eaten regularly, but egg yolk is limited in this diet. Egg yolk should be limited to four per week to help to control your saturated fat intake. Though, egg whites can be eaten much more often.

Legumes

The importance of legumes is also emphasized in the Mediterranean diet. These include beans, peas, lentils and snap peas. Legumes have a high fiber and protein count which is a great addition to your diet.

Foods to Avoid

You should reduce red meat in the Mediterranean diet since it can contribute to heart disease, but you don't have to completely avoid it. With this diet, you don't have to completely avoid anything, but there are certain items that should be reduced and eaten sparingly. When you want to eat something like red meat, try to choose a small portion of lean red meat instead, and keep it down to three to four times per month. Here are some more foods to limit or avoid all together if possible.

- *Added Sugars:* This includes candies, ice cream, table sugar and soda.
- *Refined Grains:* This includes pasta that's made of refined wheat and white bread.
- *Trans Fat:* This can be found in various processed foods, but it's also in margarine!
- *Refined Oils:* This includes cottonseed oil, vegetable oil, canola oil and soybean oil.
- *Processed Meats:* Some common examples are processed hot dogs and sausages.

- *Highly Processed Foods:* This includes anything that is labeled "diet", "low fat" or was obviously made in a factory. Remember that you should be concentrating on whole, natural ingredients.

Swapping Food Out

If you're trying to stick to a Mediterranean diet, you need to know what common food you're eating can be swapped with to help keep you on track.

- *Butter:* Just swap it out for olive oil.
- *Salt:* Just swap it out for a variety of herbs and spices instead.
- *Mayonnaise:* Mayonnaise can be swapped out for mashed avocado.
- *Beer:* It's better to switch to a glass or two of red wine which has heart benefits.
- *Beef:* Beef isn't great for you, but you can usually swap it out for salmon which can easily be found at most grocery stores.
- *Potato Chips:* Instead of munching on something that has no health benefits, choose a bag of mixed nuts. Just make sure they're unsalted.
- *Jam or Jelly:* Swap it out for fresh fruit instead. You may want to even puree it in a food processor.
- *Rice or Bread:* While you can eat whole wheat bread and some rice on the Mediterranean diet, cut it back. If you're trying to cut back try to switch for legumes instead.

- *Cakes & Cookies:* Try vegetables and hummus for a healthy alternative that will curb your appetite.

The Take Away

Now that you know what you should and shouldn't eat, you need to make sure that you avoid as much temptation as possible. Clean out your home from things that are too unhealthy, especially at the beginning of your dietary change. It can be hard to stick to a lifestyle change. You'll also need to keep in mind your portion control, and you'll need to start making some time for physical activity even if it's just twenty minutes a day.

Chapter 9. Planning Your Mediterranean Diet

Proper preparation guarantees success at the end. Deciding to follow the Mediterranean diet program will not help you if there are internal flaws. If you have access to a dietician, then consult with him/her. The expert will chart out a watertight food plan that will give you the gifts of health and physical wellbeing. Thanks to food magazines, online articles, and blogs, even a beginner will be able to identify the critical points of the Mediterranean Diet.

A proportionate combination of elements

A novice may think that the Mediterranean diet is all about munching on green salads, with olive oil dressing and taking sips of red wine. Though there is a difference between the western and the European cooking styles, these people understand the importance of a balanced meal. Your body needs carbohydrates, fats, proteins, roughage, and minerals to stay in top shape. Absence of any of these nutritional elements will make you internally weak.

A close look at the Mediterranean Diet pyramid ensures that every meal you have contains all elements in a balanced proportion. If you are not good with numbers and measurements, the simplest way is to divide the plate into three parts. Fill half of it with fruits and veggies, while one-quarter will be composed of assorted whole grains. The remaining one-quarter will contain lean meat, especially fish.

Understand the importance of whole products

No Mediterranean household invests money in processed foods. Processed foods are chemically treated in the factories to enhance their appearance. In the process, the nutritional value gets depleted drastically. The Mediterranean diet stresses the use of whole products, like vegetables, nuts, legumes, nuts, and whole grains.

Elements to be considered by Mediterranean Diet enthusiasts

Binge on veggies – The key feature of this diet is fresh fruits and vegetables. People in the Mediterranean areas depend on fresh farm products only. This diet plan consists of anything between seven and ten fruit-veggies servings on a daily basis. The high percentage of veggies and fruits will put a stopper on heart-related ailments. You don't have to sit with a bowl of vegetables and assorted fruit mixtures every time you feel hungry. Simply adding some spinach to your morning omelet or loading avocados onto your evening sandwich will do the trick. Apple slices, with nuts, will substitute for an unhealthy burger.

Replace meat with fresh fish – Lack of protein in the diet will impair the development of our muscles. In the Mediterranean diet, people stress eating fatty fish instead of red meat. Too much consumption of red meat will pave the path for high BP and heart diseases.

To attain protein, you will have to depend on fish like mackerel, salmon, herring, and tuna. Apart from being protein-rich, these are also potential sources of Omega-3 fatty acids. It will keep any inflammation under check and will also boost up the good cholesterol levels. Shellfish are also included in this diet plan. These are considered functional lean proteins. Additionally, turkey meat, chicken, and eggs are common ingredients in Mediterranean dishes.

Swap processed butter with olive oil – While most other diet plans stress the core ingredients, the cooking medium is also considered necessary in the Mediterranean diet. The type of fat obtained from olive oil will not create a negative impact on the cardiovascular system. Additionally, it will also come in handy to help manage body weight.

Go for healthy dairy products – A dollop of cheese has the power to enhance the flavor of any dish. But processed cheese will harm the heart and increase body fat drastically. Thus, the Mediterranean diet supplements this with natural dairy products. Naturally manufactured flavored cheeses, for instance, Parmesan or feta will intensify the flavors sans the adverse effects. Fermented or plain Greek yogurts are also standard on this diet list. Consuming such milk products makes it easy for the body to break them down and allows for better absorption.

Pick whole grains – Whole grains are another essential part of the Mediterranean diet. If you think that munching on unprocessed nuts will increase your body weight, then it is time to shun the thought forever. Most types of nuts used in this diet program contain healthy fats. Other whole cereals will ensure that blood sugar, blood pressure, cholesterol and sugar levels stay within the normal ranges. Consuming unprocessed whole grains will increase Vitamin B and other fiber-based components in your body. Additionally, this fiber will also act as roughage that will ease your gut and intestinal functions.

Limit sugar intakes – Skipping sugar entirely will cause the average blood sugar level to fall. But the Mediterranean diet highlights the use of natural sugar supplements like pure honey instead of processed white sugar granules. It is best to keep its use within healthy limits. Unprocessed brown sugar is also used in Mediterranean dishes to add some sweetness.

Healthy snacking ideas – The lazy afternoons and the evenings are the perfect time for some snacks. While an average American will opt for a pizza or burger, people following the Mediterranean diet will go for an assortment of nuts and crunchy fruits. The nut-n-fruit salad, with proper dressing, will not only meet your hunger, but will add nutritional value as well.

Importance of red wine – The importance of red wine has been documented since time immemorial. The Mediterranean climate offers the ideal condition for the growth of several types of grapes. A glass of red wine is an inseparable part of any Mediterranean meal. Red wine is good for heart, blood circulation, kidney, stomach, and skin. Two glasses of wine with lunch and dinner will make your Mediterranean diet complete.

Chapter 10. 21-Day Meal Plan

DAY	BREAKFAST	LUNCH	DINNER	SNACK/DESSERT
1	BREAKFAST EGG ON AVOCADO	ITALIAN LAMB SHANKS	STUFFED SARDINES	MEDITERRANEAN FLATBREAD WITH TOPPINGS
2	BREAKFAST EGG-ARTICHOKE CASSEROLE	BEEF GOULASH	MINI GREEK MEATLOAVES	SMOKED SALMON AND GOAT CHEESE BITES
3	BREKKY EGG-POTATO HASH	INSTANT POT KOREAN BEEF	YOGURT-AND-HERB-MARINATED PORK TENDERLOIN	MEDITERRANEAN CHICKPEA BOWL
4	DILL AND TOMATO FRITTATA	BEEF RAGU	ROSEMARY POTATOES	HUMMUS SNACK BOWL
5	PALEO ALMOND BANANA PANCAKES	SLOPPY JOE WITH BEEF	DELICIOUS ITALIAN BELL PEPPER	CROCK-POT PALEO CHUNKY MIX
6	BANANA-COCONUT BREAKFAST	BEEF & TOMATO SOUP	PESTO ZUCCHINI	SMOKED EGGPLANT DIP

7	BASIL AND TOMATO SOUP	GROUND LAMB CURRY	PESTO CAULIFLOWER	PUMPKIN CREAM
8	BUTTERNUT SQUASH HUMMUS	ROSEMARY LAMB	ITALIAN TOMATO MUSHROOMS	ITALIAN OVEN ROASTED VEGETABLES
9	CAJUN JAMBALAYA SOUP	THYME LAMB	CHICKPEA & POTATO	GREEK SPINACH YOGURT ARTICHOKE DIP
10	COLLARD GREEN WRAP GREEK STYLE	GARLIC LAMB SHANKS WITH PORT	ZESTY GREEN BEANS	SAUTÉED APRICOTS
11	PORTOBELLO MUSHROOM PIZZA	SEA BASS IN A PAN WITH PEPPERS	WALNUT-ROSEMARY CRUSTED SALMON	SPICED KALE CHIPS
12	ROASTED ROOT VEGGIES	CRUSTY TUNA PATTIES	CAPRESE STUFFED PORTOBELLO MUSHROOMS	YOGURT DIP
13	AMAZINGLY GOOD	BAKED TERIYAKI SALMON	GREEK SALAD NACHOS	ZUCCHINI FRITTERS

	PARSLEY TABBOULEH			
14	APPETIZING MUSHROOM LASAGNA	WHOLE ROASTED MACKEREL	GREEK CHICKEN WITH LEMON VINAIGRETTE AND ROASTED SPRING VEGETABLES	CHIA AND BERRIES SMOOTHIE BOWL
15	ARTICHOKES, OLIVES & TUNA PASTA	WHITE FISH SAUTÉED WITH LEMON, CAPERS AND HERBS	CHICKEN IN TOMATO-BALSAMIC PAN SAUCE	CUCUMBER BITES
16	BAKED RICOTTA WITH PEARS	BAKED FISH WITH OLIVES, TOMATOES, AND EGGPLANT	CHICKEN SOUVLAKI KEBABS WITH MEDITERRANEAN COUSCOUS	STUFFED AVOCADO
17	MEDITERRANEAN FRUIT BULGUR	GRILLED WHITE FISH	CAPRESE CHICKEN	WRAPPED PLUMS

	BREAKFAST BOWL	WITH FRESH BASIL PESTO	HASSELBACK STYLE	
18	SCRAMBLED EGGS WITH GOAT CHEESE AND ROASTED PEPPERS	WHITE FISH WITH CHICKPEAS AND CHORIZO	SIMPLE GRILLED SALMON WITH VEGGIES	CUCUMBER SANDWICH BITES
19	MARINARA EGGS WITH PARSLEY	FRESH SALMON WITH LEMON BUTTER AND NEW POTATOES	GREEK TURKEY BURGERS WITH SPINACH, FETA &TZATZIKI	CUCUMBER ROLLS
20	ITALIAN BREAKFAST BRUSCHETTA	FRESH FISH PUTTANESCA SALAD WITH COUSCOUS	MEDITERRANEAN CHICKEN QUINOA BOWL	OLIVES AND CHEESE STUFFED TOMATOES
21	JULENE'S GREEN JUICE	TUNA CROQUETTES	CREAMY DILL POTATOES	CRÈME CARAMEL

Chapter 11. Breakfast & Brunch Recipes

Breakfast Egg on Avocado

Preparation Time: 10 minutes

Cooking Time: 15 minutes

Servings: 6 ,

Ingredients:

1 tsp garlic powder

1/2 tsp sea salt

1/4 cup Parmesan cheese (grated or shredded)

1/4 tsp black pepper

3 medium avocados (cut in half, pitted, skin on)

6 medium eggs

Directions: Prepare muffin tins and preheat the oven to 350oF. To ensure that the egg would fit inside the cavity of the avocado, lightly scrape off 1/3 of the meat. Place avocado on muffin tin to ensure that it faces with the top up. Evenly season each avocado with pepper, salt, and garlic powder. Add one egg on each avocado cavity and garnish tops with cheese. Pop in the oven and bake until the egg white is set, about 15 minutes. Serve and enjoy.

Nutrition: Calories: 252 Protein: 14.0g Carbs: 4.0g Fat: 20.0g

Breakfast Egg-artichoke Casserole

Preparation Time: 8 minutes

Cooking Time: 35 minutes

Servings: 8

Ingredients:

16 large eggs

14 ounce can artichoke hearts, drained

10-ounce box frozen chopped spinach, thawed and drained well

1 cup shredded white cheddar

1 garlic clove, minced

1 teaspoon salt

1/2 cup parmesan cheese

1/2 cup ricotta cheese

1/2 teaspoon dried thyme

1/2 teaspoon crushed red pepper

1/4 cup milk

1/4 cup shaved onion

Directions:

Lightly grease a 9x13-inch baking dish with cooking spray and preheat the oven to 350oF.

In a large mixing bowl, add eggs and milk. Mix thoroughly.

With a paper towel, squeeze out the excess moisture from the spinach leaves and add to the bowl of eggs.

Into small pieces, break the artichoke hearts and separate the leaves. Add to the bowl of eggs.

Except for the ricotta cheese, add remaining ingredients in the bowl of eggs and mix thoroughly.

Pour egg mixture into the prepared dish.

Evenly add dollops of ricotta cheese on top of the eggs and then pop in the oven.

Bake until eggs are set and doesn't jiggle when shook, about 35 minutes.

Remove from the oven and evenly divide into suggested servings. Enjoy.

Nutrition:

Calories: 302

Protein: 22.6g

Carbs: 10.8g

Fat: 18.7g

Brekky Egg-potato Hash

Preparation Time: 5 minutes

Cooking Time: 25 minutes

Servings: 2

Ingredients:

1 zucchini, diced

1/2 cup chicken broth

½ pound cooked chicken

1 tablespoon olive oil

4 ounces shrimp

Salt and ground black pepper to taste

1 large sweet potato, diced

2 eggs

1/4 teaspoon cayenne pepper

2 teaspoons garlic powder

1 cup fresh spinach (optional)

Directions:

In a skillet, add the olive oil.

Fry the shrimp, cooked chicken and sweet potato for 2 minutes.

Add the cayenne pepper, garlic powder and salt, and toss for 4 minutes.

Add the zucchini and toss for another 3 minutes.

Whisk the eggs in a bowl and add to the skillet.

Season using salt and pepper. Cover with the lid.

Cook for 1 minute and add the chicken broth.

Cover and cook for another 8 minutes on high heat.

Add the spinach and toss for 2 more minutes.

Serve immediately.

Nutrition:

Calories: 190

Protein: 11.7g

Carbs: 2.9g

Fat: 12.3g

Dill and Tomato Frittata

Preparation Time: 10 minutes

Cooking Time: 35 minutes

Servings: 6

Ingredients:

Pepper and salt to taste

1 tsp red pepper flakes

2 garlic cloves, minced

½ cup crumbled goat cheese – optional

2 tbsp fresh chives, chopped

2 tbsp fresh dill, chopped

4 tomatoes, diced

8 eggs, whisked

1 tsp coconut oil

Directions:

Grease a 9-inch round baking pan and preheat oven to 325oF.

In a large bowl, mix well all ingredients and pour into prepped pan.

Pop into the oven and bake until middle is cooked through around 30-35 minutes.

Remove from oven and garnish with more chives and dill.

Nutrition:

Calories: 149

Protein: 13.26g

Carbs: 9.93g

Fat: 10.28g

Paleo Almond Banana Pancakes

Preparation Time: 10 minutes

Cooking Time: 10 minutes

Servings: 3

Ingredients:

¼ cup almond flour

½ teaspoon ground cinnamon

3 eggs

1 banana, mashed

1 tablespoon almond butter

1 teaspoon vanilla extract

1 teaspoon olive oil

Sliced banana to serve

Directions:

Whisk the eggs in a mixing bowl until they become fluffy.

In another bowl, mash the banana using a fork and add to the egg mixture.

Add the vanilla, almond butter, cinnamon and almond flour.

Mix into a smooth batter.

Heat the olive oil in a skillet.

Add one spoonful of the batter and fry them on both sides.

Keep doing these steps until you are done with all the batter.

Add some sliced banana on top before serving.

Nutrition:

Calories: 306

Protein: 14.4g

Carbs: 3.6g

Fat: 26.0g

Banana-Coconut Breakfast

Preparation Time: 10 minutes

Cooking Time: 3 minutes

Servings: 4

Ingredients:

1 ripe banana

1 cup desiccated coconut

1 cup coconut milk

3 tablespoons raisins, chopped

2 tablespoon ground flax seed

1 teaspoon vanilla

A dash of cinnamon

A dash of nutmeg

Salt to taste

Directions:

Place all ingredients in a deep pan.

Allow to simmer for 3 minutes on low heat.

Place in individual containers.

Put a label and store in the fridge.

Allow to thaw at room temperature before heating in the microwave oven.

Nutrition:

Calories:279

Carbs: 25.46g

Protein: 6.4g

Fat: g

Fiber: 5.9g

Basil and Tomato Soup

Preparation Time: 10 minutes

Cooking Time: 25 minutes

Servings: 2

Ingredients:

Salt and pepper to taste

2 bay leaves

1 ½ cups almond milk, unsweetened

½ tsp raw apple cider vinegar

1/3 cup basil leaves

¼ cup tomato paste

3 cups tomatoes, chopped

1 medium celery stalk, chopped

1 medium carrot, chopped

1 medium garlic clove, minced

½ cup white onion

2 tbsp vegetable broth

Directions:

Heat the vegetable broth in a large saucepan over medium heat.

Add the onions and cook for 3 minutes. Add the garlic and cook for another minute.

Add the celery and carrots and cook for 1 minute.

Mix in the tomatoes and bring to a boil. Simmer for 15 minutes.

Add the almond milk, basil and bay leaves. Season with salt and pepper to taste.

Nutrition:

Calories: 213

Carbs: 42.0g

Protein: 6.9g

Fat: 3.9g

Butternut Squash Hummus

Preparation Time: 10 minutes

Cooking Time: 15 minutes

Servings: 8

Ingredients:

2 pounds butternut squash, seeded and peeled

1 tablespoon olive oil

¼ cup tahini

2 tablespoons lemon juice

2 cloves of garlic, minced

Salt and pepper to taste

Directions:

Heat the oven to 3000F.

Coat the butternut squash with olive oil.

Place in a baking dish and bake for 15 minutes in the oven.

Once the squash is cooked, place in a food processor together with the rest of the ingredients.

Pulse until smooth.

Place in individual containers.

Put a label and store in the fridge.

Allow to warm at room temperature before heating in the microwave oven.

Serve with carrots or celery sticks.

Nutrition:

Calories: 115

Carbs: 15.8g

Protein: 2.5g

Fat:5.8gFiber: 6.7g

Cajun Jambalaya Soup

Preparation Time: 10 minutes

Cooking Time: 6 hours

Servings: 6

Ingredients:

¼ cup Frank's red hot sauce

3 tbsp Cajun seasoning

2 cups okra

½ head of cauliflower

1 pkg spicy Andouille sausages

4 oz chicken, diced

1 lb. large shrimps, raw and deveined

2 bay leaves

2 cloves garlic, diced

1 large can organic diced tomatoes

1 large onion, chopped

4 pepper

5 cups chicken stock

Directions:

In slow cooker, place the bay leaves, red hot sauce, Cajun seasoning, chicken, garlic, onions, and peppers.

Set slow cooker on low and cook for 5 ½ hours.

Then add sausages cook for 10 minutes.

Meanwhile, pulse cauliflower in food processor to make cauliflower rice.

Add cauliflower rice into slow cooker. Cook for 20 minutes.

Serve and enjoy.

Nutrition:

Calories: 155

Carbs: 13.9g

Protein: 17.4g

Fat: 3.8g

Collard Green Wrap Greek Style

Preparation Time: 10 minutes

Cooking Time: 0 minutes

Servings: 4

Ingredients:

½ block feta, cut into 4 (1-inch thick) strips (4-oz)

½ cup purple onion, diced

½ medium red bell pepper, julienned

1 medium cucumber, julienned

4 large cherry tomatoes, halved

4 large collard green leaves, washed

8 whole kalamata olives, halved

1 cup full-fat plain Greek yogurt

1 tablespoon white vinegar

1 teaspoon garlic powder

2 tablespoons minced fresh dill

2 tablespoons olive oil

2.5-ounces cucumber, seeded and grated (¼-whole)

Salt and pepper to taste

Directions:

Make the Tzatziki sauce first: make sure to squeeze out all the excess liquid from the cucumber after grating. In a small bowl, mix all sauce ingredients thoroughly and refrigerate.

Prepare and slice all wrap ingredients.

On a flat surface, spread one collard green leaf. Spread 2 tablespoons of Tzatziki sauce on middle of the leaf.

Layer ¼ of each of the tomatoes, feta, olives, onion, pepper, and cucumber. Place them on the center of the leaf, like piling them high instead of spreading them.

Fold the leaf like you would a burrito. Repeat process for remaining ingredients.

Serve and enjoy.

Nutrition:

Calories: 165.3

Protein: 7.0g

Carbs: 9.9g

Fat: 11.2g

Portobello Mushroom Pizza

Preparation Time: 10 minutes

Cooking Time: 12 minutes

Servings: 4

Ingredients:

½ teaspoon red pepper flakes

A handful of fresh basil, chopped

1 can black olives, chopped

1 medium onion, chopped

1 green pepper, chopped

¼ cup chopped roasted yellow peppers

½ cup prepared nut cheese, shredded

2 cups prepared gluten-free pizza sauce

8 Portobello mushrooms, cleaned and stems removed

Directions:

Preheat the oven toaster.

Take a baking sheet and grease it. Set aside.

Place the Portobello mushroom cap-side down and spoon 2 tablespoon of packaged pizza sauce on the underside of each cap. Add nut cheese and top with the remaining ingredients.

Broil for 12 minutes or until the toppings are wilted.

Nutrition:

Calories: 578

Carbs: 73.0g

Protein: 24.4g

Fat: 22.4g

Roasted Root Veggies

Preparation Time: 10 minutes

Cooking Time: 1 hour and 30 minutes

Servings: 6

Ingredients:

2 tbsp olive oil

1 head garlic, cloves separated and peeled

1 large turnip, peeled and cut into ½-inch pieces

1 medium sized red onion, cut into ½-inch pieces

1 ½ lbs. beets, trimmed but not peeled, scrubbed and cut into ½-inch pieces

1 ½ lbs. Yukon gold potatoes, unpeeled, cut into ½-inch pieces

2 ½ lbs. butternut squash, peeled, seeded, cut into ½-inch pieces

Directions:

Grease 2 rimmed and large baking sheets. Preheat oven to 425oF. In a large bowl, mix all ingredients thoroughly. Into the two baking sheets, evenly divide the root vegetables, spread in one layer. Season generously with pepper and salt. Pop into the oven and roast for 1 hour and 15 minute or until golden brown and tender. Remove from oven and let it cool for at least 15 minutes before serving.

Nutrition: Calories: 298 Carbs: 61.1g Protein: 7.4g Fat: 5.0g

Amazingly Good Parsley Tabbouleh

Preparation Time: 10 minutes

Cooking Time: 15 minutes

Servings: 4

Ingredients:

¼ cup chopped fresh mint

¼ cup lemon juice

¼ tsp salt

½ cup bulgur

½ tsp minced garlic

1 cup water

1 small cucumber, peeled, seeded and diced

2 cups finely chopped flat-leaf parsley

2 tbsp extra virgin olive oil

2 tomatoes, diced

4 scallions, thinly sliced

Pepper to taste

Directions:

Cook bulgur according to package instructions. Drain and set aside to cool for at least 15 minutes.

In a small bowl, mix pepper, salt, garlic, oil, and lemon juice.

Transfer bulgur into a large salad bowl and mix in scallions, cucumber, tomatoes, mint, and parsley.

Pour in dressing and toss well to coat.

Place bowl in ref until chilled before serving.

Nutrition:

Calories: 134.8

Carbs: 13g

Protein: 7.2g

Fat: 6g

Appetizing Mushroom Lasagna

Preparation Time: 10 minutes

Cooking Time: 75 minutes

Servings: 8

Ingredients:

½ cup grated Parmigiano-Reggiano cheese

No boil lasagna noodles

Cooking spray

¼ cup all-purpose flour

3 cups reduced fat milk, divided

2 tbsp chopped fresh chives, divided

1/3 cup less fat cream cheese

½ cup white wine

6 garlic cloves, minced and divided

1 ½ tbsp. Chopped fresh thyme

½ tsp freshly ground black pepper, divided

1 tsp salt, divided

1 package 4 oz pre-sliced exotic mushroom blend

1 package 8oz pre-sliced cremini mushrooms

1 ¼ cups chopped shallots

2 tbsp olive oil, divided

1 tbsp butter

1 oz dried porcini mushrooms

1 cup boiling water

Directions:

For 30 minutes, submerge porcini in 1 cup boiling hot water. With a sieve, strain mushroom and reserve liquid.

Over medium high fire, melt butter on a fry pan. Mix in 2 tbsp oil and for three minutes fry shallots. Add ¼ tsp pepper, ½ tsp salt, exotic mushrooms and cremini, cook for six minutes. Stir in 3 garlic cloves and thyme, cook for a minute. Bring to a boil as you pour wine by increasing fire to high and cook until liquid evaporates around a minute. Turn off fire and stir in porcini mushrooms, 1 tbsp chives and cream cheese. Mix well.

On medium high fire, place a separate medium sized pan with 1 tbsp oil. Sauté for half a minute 3 garlic cloves. Then bring to a boil as you pour 2 ¾ cups milk and reserved porcini liquid. Season with remaining pepper and salt. In a separate bowl, whisk together flour and ¼ cup milk and pour into pan. Stir constantly and cook until mixture thickens.

In a greased rectangular glass dish, pour and spread ½ cup of sauce, top with lasagna, top with half of mushroom mixture and another layer of lasagna. Repeat the layering process and instead of lasagna layer, end with the mushroom mixture and cover with cheese.

For 45 minutes, bake the lasagna in a preheated 350oF oven. Garnish with chives before serving.

Nutrition:

Calories: 268

Carbs: 29.6g Protein: 10.2g Fat: 12.6g

Artichokes, Olives & Tuna Pasta

Preparation Time: 10 minutes

Cooking Time: 15 minutes

Servings: 4

Ingredients:

¼ cup chopped fresh basil

¼ cup chopped green olives

¼ tsp freshly ground pepper

½ cup white wine

½ tsp salt, divided

1 10-oz package frozen artichoke hearts, thawed and squeezed dry

2 cups grape tomatoes, halved

2 tbsp lemon juice

2 tsp chopped fresh rosemary

2 tsp freshly grated lemon zest

3 cloves garlic, minced

4 tbsp extra virgin olive oil, divided

6-oz whole wheat penne pasta

8-oz tuna steak, cut into 3 pieces

Directions:

Cook penne pasta according to package instructions. Drain and set aside.

Preheat grill to medium high.

In bowl, toss and mix ¼ tsp pepper, ¼ tsp salt, 1 tsp rosemary, lemon zest, 1 tbsp oil and tuna pieces.

Grill tuna for 3 minutes per side. Allow to cool and flake into bite sized pieces.

On medium fire, place a large nonstick saucepan and heat 3 tbsp oil.

Sauté remaining rosemary, garlic olives, and artichoke hearts for 4 minutes

Add wine and tomatoes, bring to a boil and cook for 3 minutes while stirring once in a while.

Add remaining salt, lemon juice, tuna pieces and pasta. Cook until heated through.

To serve, garnish with basil and enjoy.

Nutrition:

Calories: 127.6

Carbs: 13g

Protein: 7.2g

Fat: 5.2g

Baked Ricotta With Pears

Preparation Time: 5 minutes

Cooking Time: 25 minutes

Servings: 4

Ingredients:

Nonstick cooking spray

1 (16-ounce) container whole-milk ricotta cheese

2 large eggs

¼ cup white whole-wheat flour or whole-wheat pastry flour

1 tablespoon sugar

1 teaspoon vanilla extract

¼ teaspoon ground nutmeg

1 pear, cored and diced

2 tablespoons water

1 tablespoon honey

Directions:

Preheat the oven to 400°F. Spray four 6-ounce ramekins with nonstick cooking spray.

In a large bowl, beat together the ricotta, eggs, flour, sugar, vanilla, and nutmeg. Spoon into the ramekins. Bake for 22 to 25 minutes, or until the ricotta is just about set. Remove from the oven and cool slightly on racks.

While the ricotta is baking, in a small saucepan over medium heat, simmer the pear in the water for 10 minutes, until slightly softened. Remove from the heat, and stir in the honey.

Serve the ricotta ramekins topped with the warmed pear.

Nutrition:

Calories: 312

Total Fat: 17g

Saturated Fat: 10g

Cholesterol: 163mg

Sodium: 130mg

Total Carbohydrates: 23g

Fiber: 2g Protein: 17g

Mediterranean Fruit Bulgur Breakfast Bowl

Preparation Time: 5 minutes

Cooking Time: 15 minutes

Servings: 6

Ingredients:

1½ cups uncooked bulgur

2 cups 2% milk

1 cup water

½ teaspoon ground cinnamon

2 cups frozen (or fresh, pitted) dark sweet cherries

8 dried (or fresh) figs, chopped

½ cup chopped almonds

¼ cup loosely packed fresh mint, chopped

Warm 2% milk, for serving (optional)

Directions:

In a medium saucepan, combine the bulgur, milk, water, and cinnamon. Stir once, then bring just to a boil. Cover, reduce the heat to medium-low, and simmer for 10 minutes or until the liquid is absorbed.

Turn off the heat, but keep the pan on the stove, and stir in the frozen cherries (no need to thaw), figs, and almonds. Stir well, cover for 1 minute, and let the hot bulgur thaw the cherries and partially hydrate the figs. Stir in the mint.

Scoop into serving bowls. Serve with warm milk, if desired. You can also serve it chilled.

Nutrition:

Calories: 301

Total Fat: 6g

Saturated Fat: 1g

Cholesterol: 7mg

Sodium: 40mg

Total Carbohydrates: 57g

Fiber: 9g

Protein: 9g

Scrambled Eggs With Goat Cheese And Roasted Peppers

Preparation Time: 5 minutes

Cooking Time: 10 minutes

Servings: 4

Ingredients:

1½ teaspoons extra-virgin olive oil

1 cup chopped bell peppers, any color (about 1 medium pepper)

2 garlic cloves, minced (about 1 teaspoon)

6 large eggs

¼ teaspoon kosher or sea salt

2 tablespoons water

½ cup crumbled goat cheese (about 2 ounces)

2 tablespoons loosely packed chopped fresh mint

Directions:

In a large skillet over medium-high heat, heat the oil. Add the peppers and cook for 5 minutes, stirring occasionally. Add the garlic and cook for 1 minute.

While the peppers are cooking, in a medium bowl, whisk together the eggs, salt, and water.

Turn the heat down to medium-low. Pour the egg mixture over the peppers. Let the eggs cook undisturbed for 1 to 2 minutes, until they begin to set on the bottom. Sprinkle with the goat cheese.

Cook the eggs for about 1 to 2 more minutes, stirring slowly, until the eggs are soft-set and custardy. (They will continue to cook off the stove from the residual heat in the pan.)

Top with the fresh mint and serve.

Nutrition:

Calories: 201

Total Fat: 15g

Saturated Fat: 6g

Cholesterol: 294mg

Sodium: 176mg

Total Carbohydrates: 5g Fiber: 2g Protein: 15g

Marinara Eggs With Parsley

Preparation Time: 5 minutes

Cooking Time: 15 minutes

Servings: 6

Ingredients:

1 tablespoon extra-virgin olive oil

1 cup chopped onion (about ½ medium onion)

2 garlic cloves, minced (about 1 teaspoon)

2 (14.5-ounce) cans Italian diced tomatoes, undrained, no salt added

6 large eggs

½ cup chopped fresh flat-leaf (Italian) parsley

Crusty Italian bread and grated Parmesan or Romano cheese, for serving (optional)

Directions:

In a large skillet over medium-high heat, heat the oil. Add the onion and cook for 5 minutes, stirring occasionally. Add the garlic and cook for 1 minute.

Pour the tomatoes with their juices over the onion mixture and cook until bubbling, 2 to 3 minutes. While waiting for the tomato mixture to bubble, crack one egg into a small custard cup or coffee mug.

When the tomato mixture bubbles, lower the heat to medium. Then use a large spoon to make six indentations in the tomato mixture. Gently pour the first cracked egg into one indentation and repeat, cracking the remaining eggs, one at a time, into the custard cup and pouring one into each indentation. Cover the skillet and cook for 6 to 7 minutes, or until the eggs are done to your liking (about 6 minutes for soft-cooked, 7 minutes for harder cooked).

Top with the parsley, and serve with the bread and grated cheese, if desired.

Nutrition:

Calories: 122

Total Fat: 7g

Saturated Fat: 2g

Cholesterol: 186mg

Sodium: 207mg

Total Carbohydrates: 7g Fiber: 1g Protein: 7g

Italian Breakfast Bruschetta

Preparation Time: 10 minutes

Cooking Time: 20 minutes

Servings: 4

Ingredients:

¼ teaspoon kosher or sea salt

6 cups broccoli rabe, stemmed and chopped (about 1 bunch)

1 tablespoon extra-virgin olive oil

2 garlic cloves, minced (about 1 teaspoon)

1 ounce prosciutto, cut or torn into ½-inch pieces

¼ teaspoon crushed red pepper

Nonstick cooking spray

3 large eggs

1 tablespoon 2% milk

¼ teaspoon freshly ground black pepper

4 teaspoons grated Parmesan or Pecorino Romano cheese

1 garlic clove, halved

8 (¾-inch-thick) slices baguette-style whole-grain bread or 4 slices larger Italian-style whole-grain bread

Directions:

Bring a large stockpot of water to a boil. Add the salt and broccoli rabe, and boil for 2 minutes. Drain in a colander. In a large skillet over medium heat, heat the oil. Add the garlic, prosciutto, and crushed red pepper, and cook for 2 minutes, stirring often. Add the broccoli rabe and cook for an additional 3 minutes, stirring a few times. Transfer to a bowl and set aside. Place the skillet back on the stove over low heat and coat with nonstick cooking spray. In a small bowl, whisk together the eggs, milk, and pepper. Pour into the skillet. Stir and cook until the eggs are soft scrambled, 3 to 5 minutes. Add the broccoli rabe mixture back to the skillet along with the cheese. Stir and cook for about 1 minute, until heated through. Remove from the heat.

Toast the bread, then rub the cut sides of the garlic clove halves onto one side of each slice of the toast. (Save the garlic for another recipe.) Spoon the egg mixture onto each piece of toast and serve.

Nutrition: Calories: 216 Total Fat: 9g

Saturated Fat: 2g Cholesterol: 145mg Sodium: 522mg

Total Carbohydrates: 20g Fiber: 5g Protein: 13g

Julene's Green Juice

Preparation Time: 5 minutes

Cooking Time: 0 minutes

Servings: 1

Ingredients:

3 cups dark leafy greens

1 cucumber

¼ cup fresh Italian parsley leaves

¼ pineapple, cut into wedges

½ green apple

½ orange - ½ lemon

Pinch grated fresh ginger

Directions: Using a juicer, run the greens, cucumber, parsley, pineapple, apple, orange, lemon, and ginger through it, pour into a large cup, and serve.

Nutrition: Calories: 108

Protein: 11g Total Carbohydrates: 29g Fiber: 9g Total Fat: 2g

Chapter 12. Lunch Recipes

Italian Lamb Shanks

Preparation Time: 15 minutes

Cooking Time: 60 minutes

Servings: 4

Ingredients:

3 lbs. lamb shanks

4 cloves garlic, minced

3 stalks celery, diced

1 cup beef stock

1 tablespoon balsamic vinegar

1 tablespoon coconut oil

1 tablespoon tomato paste

1 yellow onion, diced

½ teaspoon crushed red pepper flakes

½ teaspoon salt

¼ teaspoon black pepper

1 can (14-ounces) fire-roasted tomatoes

3 carrots, peeled and chopped

Italian parsley, fresh, chopped for garnish

Directions:

Sprinkle lamb shanks with pepper and salt. Set your instant pot to the sauté mode, add the coconut oil and heat.

Add the lamb shanks to hot coconut oil and cook for about 10-minutes or until all sides are brown.

Transfer to a platter when sides are browned.

Add garlic, celery, onion, and carrots to instant pot. Use salt and pepper to season, cook until the onion becomes translucent—stirring often.

Add the fire-roasted tomatoes and tomato paste. Stir to blend.

Return the lamb shanks to the pot. Add the beef stock and balsamic vinegar.

Cancel the sauté mode, and cover pot with lid and secure it.

Set the pot to Manual mode, on high, with a cook time of 45-minutes.

When the cook time is completed, release the pressure naturally for 15-minutes.

Transfer the lamb shanks to a serving plate. Ladle sauce over lamb shanks.

Garnish with fresh, chopped parsley and enjoy warm!

Nutrition:

Calories: 257   Total Fat: 11g   Carbs: 9g   Protein: 28g

Beef Goulash

Preparation Time: 15 minutes

Cooking Time: 15 minutes

Servings: 6

Ingredients:

2 lbs. extra lean ground beef

2 tablespoons of sweet paprika

1 tablespoon garlic, minced

1 large sized onion, cut into strips

1 large sized red bell pepper, stemmed and seeded, cut into strips

2 teaspoons olive oil

2 cans of petite tomatoes, diced

4 cups beef stock

½ teaspoon hot paprika

Directions:

Set to your sauté mode and add 2 tablespoons olive oil.

Add ground beef to the pot and keep cooking and stirring until it breaks.

Once the beef is browned, transfer it to another bowl. Slice the stem of the pepper and deseed them. Cut them into strips.

Cut the onions into short strips.

Add teaspoon olive oil to the pot and add onion and pepper.

Add minced garlic, sweet paprika, and cook for 3-minutes.

Add beef stock and tomatoes.

Add ground beef and close and secure the lid, cook on low pressure for 15-minutes on the SOUP mode.

Use the quick-release when cooking is completed.

Serve hot and enjoy!

Nutrition:

Calories: 283

Total Fat: 13g

Carbs: 14g

Protein: 30g

Instant Pot Korean Beef

Preparation Time: 15 minutes

Cooking Time: 6 hours

Servings: 6

Ingredients:

4lbs. roast, cut into strips

¼ teaspoon salt

¼ teaspoon black pepper

1 cup chicken broth

4 tablespoons soy sauce

¼ teaspoon garlic paste

¼ teaspoon ginger

1 pear, chopped

2 cups orange juice

1 tablespoon honey

Directions:

Trim extra fat off the roast, rinse and fully dry.

Season roast with salt and pepper. Set aside.

Set the instant pot to the sauté mode, add olive oil and heat it.

Add the meat to pot and brown on all sides for about 5-minutes. Remove meat from pot and set aside. In the instant pot pour orange juice, soy sauce, garlic, ginger, pear and honey and stir to blend. Cover up the instant pot with lid and set to Manual mode, on high, for a cook time of 45-minutes. When cook time is completed, release the pressure naturally for 15-minutes. Shred the meat using two forks, then serve with rice and enjoy!

Nutrition: Calories: 490 Total Fat: 24g Carbs: 26g Protein: 41g

Beef Ragu

Preparation Time: 15 minutes

Cooking Time: 55 minutes

Servings: 6

Ingredients:

18-ounces beef chunks

2 tablespoons parsley, fresh,

Chopped, divided

2 bay leaves

2 sprigs of fresh thyme

7-ounces roasted red peppers

28-ounces crushed tomatoes

5 garlic cloves, smashed

1 teaspoon olive oil

Black pepper as needed

1 teaspoon salt

Directions:

Season the beef with salt and pepper. Set your instant pot to the sauté mode, add the oil and heat it. Cook the garlic in a pot and turn to brown.

It will take about 2-minutes, then remove garlic with slotted spoon.

Put the beef in the instant pot and cook a couple of minutes on each side. Add remaining ingredients to the pot.

Keep half of the parsley for later for garnish.

Cook the beef on manual mode, on high, for a cook time of 45-minutes.

When the cook time is completed, release the pressure naturally for 10-minutes.

Remove the bay leaves and discard them. Shred the beef using two forks.

Garnish beef with remaining parsley and serve hot with some pasta.

Nutrition:

Calories: 298

Total Fat: 11g

Carbs: 14g

Protein: 29g

Sloppy Joe with Beef

Preparation Time: 15 minutes

Cooking Time: 30 minutes

Servings: 6

Ingredients:

2 lbs. ground beef

2 tablespoons yellow mustard

2 tablespoons molasses

2 tablespoons apple cider vinegar

15-ounces tomato sauce

½ teaspoon black pepper

1 teaspoon pepper

1 teaspoon cayenne

2 teaspoons salt

2 teaspoons paprika

2 teaspoons smoked paprika

2 teaspoons cumin

8 garlic cloves, minced

2 onions, diced

2 tablespoons olive oil

Chopped cilantro, for garnishing

Directions:

Set your instant pot to the sauté mode, add oil and heat it.

Sauté, the onions in the oil for 5-minutes, then add the garlic, spices and ground beef.

Cook thoroughly until the beef turns brown. Add all the remaining ingredients, stir.

Close the lid to pot and set on the BEAN/CHILI mode, make sure the steam valve is closed.

After 30-minutes the cook time will be completed, release the pressure naturally for 10-minutes.

Serve hot.

Nutrition:

Calories: 304

Total Fat: 12g

Carbs: 16g

Protein: 28g

Beef & Tomato Soup

Preparation Time: 15 minutes

Cooking Time: 55 minutes

Servings: 6

Ingredients:

1 lb. ground beef

1 tablespoon olive oil

1 medium onion, chopped

Black pepper to taste

15-ounces beef broth

15-ounces diced tomatoes

1 teaspoon oregano, dried

1 teaspoon thyme, dried

1 tablespoon garlic, minced

Directions:

Turn your instant pot to the sauté mode, add the oil and heat it.

Add the beef to pot and cook it until it turns brown.

Add the onion, thyme, oregano, garlic and cook for an additional 3-minutes.

Add the tomatoes and beef broth and close the pot lid. Set to SOUP mode and cook for 30-minutes. When cooking is completed, release the pressure using the quick-release.

Season with salt and pepper.

Serve the soup warm.

Nutrition:

Calories: 302 Total Fat: 15g Carbs: 14g Protein: 30g

Ground Lamb Curry

Preparation Time: 15 minutes

Cooking Time: 55 minutes

Servings: 4

Ingredients:

1 lb. ground lamb

½ teaspoon Kashmiri chili powder

½ teaspoon cumin powder

1 teaspoon salt

1 teaspoon paprika

1 teaspoon meat masala, homemade

1 tablespoon coriander powder

1 onion, diced

1 cup frozen peas, rinsed

2 potatoes, chopped

1 can (13.5-ounce) tomato sauce

3 carrots, chopped

4 tomatoes, chopped

4 garlic cloves, minced

2 tablespoons ghee

1-inch fresh ginger, minced

2 Serrano peppers, minced

¼ teaspoon turmeric powder

½ teaspoon black pepper

Fresh cilantro, chopped for garnish

Directions:

Set your instant pot to the sauté mode, add the ghee and heat it. Add onions and cook them until they start to brown.

Add the garlic, ginger, Serrano pepper and stir-fry for 1-minute. Add the tomatoes. Cook for 5-minutes, then add the spice and stir-fry for 1-minute.

Add the ground lamb and cook until the meat is browned. Add the potatoes, carrots, peas, and tomato sauce. Mix well until combined.

Press the CANCEL button to stop the sauté mode.

Cover and secure the lid to the pot.

Press the CHILI button and cook for 30-minutes.

When the instant pot completes the cooking, release the pressure naturally for 15-minutes. Carefully open the lid and serve dish warm.

Nutrition: Calories: 267 Total Fat: 8g Carbs: 12g Protein: 27g

Rosemary Lamb

Preparation Time: 15 minutes

Cooking Time: 35 minutes

Servings: 6

Ingredients:

4 lbs. lamb, cubed, boneless

1 cup sliced carrots

2 tablespoons olive oil

3 tablespoons flour

6 rosemary sprigs

4 garlic cloves, minced

Salt and pepper to taste

1 ½ cups veggie stock

Directions:

Set your instant pot to the sauté mode, add the oil and heat.

Season the lamb with salt and pepper. Place lamb inside the pot with minced garlic. Cook until the lamb has browned all over. Add the flour and stir, slowly pour in the stock.

Add the rosemary and carrots, close and secure the pot lid.

Set to Manual mode, on high, with a cook time of 20-minutes.

When the cook time is completed, release the pressure naturally for 10-minutes.

Remove the rosemary stems from the pot.

Serve lamb with plenty of sauce.

Nutrition:

Calories: 272

Total Fat: 11g

Carbs: 9g

Protein: 29g

Thyme Lamb

Preparation Time: 15 minutes

Cooking Time: 55 minutes

Servings: 8

Ingredients:

1 cup fresh thyme

2 lbs. lamb

1 teaspoon oregano

1 tablespoon olive oil

1 tablespoon turmeric

¼ cup chicken stock

4 tablespoons butter

1 teaspoon sugar

¼ cup rice wine

1 teaspoon paprika

1 tablespoon ground black pepper

Directions:

Chop the fresh thyme and combine it with the oregano, ground black pepper, paprika, sugar, rice wine, chicken stock, and turmeric, mix well.

Sprinkle the lamb with the spice mixture and stir carefully.

Transfer the lamb mixture to your instant pot and add olive oil to the pot.

Close the instant pot and secure the lid, set on MEAT mode for 45-minutes.

When the cooking is completed, release the pressure naturally for 10-minutes.

Chill the lamb for a little bit before you slice it.

Serve warm or cold.

Nutrition:

Calories: 282 Total Fat: 12g Carbs: 8g Protein: 28g

Garlic Lamb Shanks with Port

Preparation Time: 15 minutes

Cooking Time: 60 minutes

Servings: 4

Ingredients:

4 lbs. lamb shanks

1 cup port wine

1 cup chicken broth

1 teaspoon rosemary, dried

2 teaspoons balsamic vinegar

2 tablespoons ghee

2 tablespoons tomato paste

20 peeled, whole garlic cloves

Salt and pepper to taste

Directions:

Trim any excess fat from lamb that you do not want, and season it generously with salt and pepper. Heat oil in your instant pot on the sauté mode.

Place the lamb into the pot, and brown it all over.

Pour in the port and stock, stir in the tomato paste and rosemary.

When the tomato paste is dissolved, close and secure the pot lid.

Set to Manual mode, on high, with a cook time of 32-minutes.

When the cook time is completed, release the pressure naturally for 10-minutes.

Remove the lamb from pot and set the pot back onto the sauté mode for about 5-minutes to thicken the sauce.

Add in vinegar and mix well.

Serve with the sauce poured over the lamb.

Nutrition:

Calories: 298

Total Fat: 13g

Carbs: 11g

Protein: 26g

Sea Bass in a Pan with Peppers

Preparation Time: 15 minutes

Cooking Time: 10 minutes

Servings: 4

Ingredients:

4 sea bass fillet, no skin

2 tablespoons olive oil (for cooking vegetables)

¼ cup olive oil (for cooking fish)

Salt, to taste

1 Red Bell Pepper, cored and chopped

1 Green Bell Pepper, cored and chopped

4 garlic cloves, minced

3 Shallots, chopped

Juice of ½ lemon

½ cup pitted Kalamata olives, chopped

½ tablespoon ground coriander

½ tablespoon garlic powder

1 teaspoon Aleppo pepper (or Sweet Spanish paprika)

1 teaspoon ground cumin

½ teaspoon black pepper

Directions:

Sprinkle fish with salt on both sides and set aside.

Combine the spices in a small bowl to make the spice mixture.

Heat two tablespoons olive oil in a medium-sized skillet over medium-high heat. Add the bell peppers, shallots, and garlic. Season with salt and 1 teaspoon of the spice mixture. Cook, stirring, for 5 minutes.

Reduce the heat, and stir in the halved olives. Leave on low heat while preparing the fish.

Pat fish dry and season with the remaining spice mixture on both sides. In a large skillet, heat ¼ cup olive oil over medium-high.

Add the fish pieces. Push down on the middle for 30 seconds or so. Cook fish on one side, until nicely browned, about 4-6 minutes.

Carefully turn fish over and cook on other side for 3-4 minutes until nicely browned. Remove fish from heat, immediately drizzle with lemon juice.

Nutrition:

Calories: 312

Protein: 11 g

Fat: 26 g

Carbs: 12 g

Crusty Tuna Patties

Preparation Time: 10 minutes

Cooking Time: 10 minutes

Servings: 4

Ingredients:

2 (5 to 6-ounce) cans tuna, drained cans

½ cup white bread, torn into pieces

2 teaspoons Dijon mustard

1 tablespoon lemon juice

1 teaspoon lemon zest

1 tablespoon water or liquid from tuna

2 tablespoons chopped fresh parsley

2 tablespoons fresh chives, green onions or shallots, chopped

Salt and pepper, to taste

1 egg

A few dashes of Tabasco or Crystal hot sauce

2 tablespoons olive oil

½ teaspoon butter

Directions:

In a medium bowl, mix the tuna, bread, mustard, lemon zest, water, lemon juice, parsley, hot sauce, chives, pepper and salt.

Mix in the egg.

Divide the mixture into four parts. Form each part into a ball and make into a patty.

Place on a wax paper lined tray and chill for one hour.

Heat a little butter and the olive oil in a stick-free or a cast iron skillet on medium high.

Place the patties in the pan carefully, and cook until nicely golden-browned, 3-4 minutes on each side.

Nutrition:

Calories: 130

Protein: 16 g

Fat: 5 g

Carbs: 5 g

Baked Teriyaki Salmon

Preparation Time: 10 minutes

Cooking Time: 20 minutes

Servings: 4

Ingredients:

4 6-ounce salmon fillets

½ white or red onion, chopped

2 bell peppers, chopped

1 cup carrots, sliced

2 cups broccoli florets

Salt and pepper, to taste

2 tablespoons oil

¼ cup soy sauce

1 cup water

2 teaspoons minced garlic

¼ cup packed brown sugar

¼ teaspoon ground ginger

2 tablespoons honey

2 teaspoons sesame seeds

¼ cup cold water

2 tablespoons corn starch

Directions:

Combine soy sauce, water, garlic, ginger, honey, and brown sugar in a medium saucepan and whisk together over medium-high heat. Bring to a boil.

Stir together corn starch and cold water until dissolved, then whisk into boiling sauce and lower heat to medium-low.

Remove from heat, stir in sesame seeds, and let the sauce cool.

Preheat the oven to 420° F.

Grease a baking sheet and place salmon filets in the center.

In a large bowl, mix vegetables with oil, tossing to coat.

Put the vegetables around the salmon. Season everything with pepper and salt.

Drizzle ⅔ of the Teriyaki sauce over the veggies and salmon. Bake for 15-20 minutes, until veggies are easily pierced with a fork and salmon is flaky and tender.

Drizzle with remaining sauce and serve immediately.

Nutrition:

Calories: 201

Protein: 21 g

Fat: 7 g

Carbs: 12 g

Whole Roasted Mackerel

Preparation Time: 5 minutes

Cooking Time: 30 minutes

Servings: 4

Ingredients:

2 whole mackerel, cleaned and gutted

5 sprigs thyme

2 lemons, thinly sliced, cut into half moons

5 sprigs oregano

2 tablespoons olive oil

Salt and pepper, to taste

Directions:

Preheat the oven to 420° F. Line a baking sheet with parchment paper and spray with cooking spray.

Score along one side of the fish. Season scored sections and the cavity with salt and pepper.

Stuff the scored sections with lemon slices, oregano, and thyme.

Stuff the cavities with herbs and remaining lemon slices

Drizzle with olive oil and roast in the oven for 20 minutes, or until golden-brown and the skin is lightly crisp.

Nutrition:

Calories: 126

Protein: 13 g Fat: 8 g   Carbs: 0.2 g

White Fish sautéed with Lemon, Capers and Herbs

Preparation Time: 10 minutes

Cooking Time: 10 minutes

Servings: 4

Ingredients:

2 Tbsp olive oil

2 Tbsp butter

4 large fresh fish fillets

Juice of 2 large lemons

3 Tbsp capers

½ cup chopped fresh parsley, mint, thyme (or any other fresh herbs you like)

Salt and pepper

Directions:

Place a non-stick pan over a medium-high heat and add the olive oil and butter, allow the butter to melt and become slightly frothy

Add the fish to the pan and fry on both sides for about 2 minutes or until golden and almost cooked through

Add the lemon juice and capers, and allow the acid of the lemon juice to deglaze the pan

Add the fresh herbs just before you remove the pan from the heat and serve

Serve with a little extra butter and a wedge of lemon!

Nutrition:

Calories: 282

Protein: 35 g

Fat: 15 g

Carbs: 3 g

Baked Fish with Olives, Tomatoes, and Eggplant

Preparation Time: 10 minutes

Cooking Time: 25 minutes

Servings: 4

Ingredients:

1 eggplant, thinly sliced

4 Tbsp olive oil

Salt and pepper

4 large, fresh white fish fillets

2 cups canned whole tomatoes

20 black olives, (remove the stones if you wish, but not crucial)

Fresh parsley

Directions:

Preheat the oven to 360 degrees Fahrenheit

Lay the eggplant into the bottom of a baking dish, and drizzle each slice with olive oil, salt and pepper and make sure each slice is coated

Pour half of the tomatoes over the eggplant

Lay the fish onto the tomatoes and add the other half of the tomatoes over the top

Scatter the olives over the tomatoes and pop the dish into the oven to bake for about 30 minutes or until the eggplant is soft and the fish is just cooked through

Serve hot, with a scattering of fresh parsley

Nutrition:

Calories: 481

Protein: 60 g

Fat: 19 g

Carbs: 15 g

Grilled White Fish with Fresh Basil Pesto

Preparation Time: 10 minutes

Cooking Time: 20 minutes

Servings: 4

Ingredients:

1 cup fresh basil leaves

4 Tbsp olive oil

¼ cup grated parmesan

¼ cup toasted pine nuts

Juice of ½ lemon

Salt and pepper

4 fresh white fish fillets

Directions:

Place the pesto ingredients into a food processor and blitz until smooth

Place the pesto into a bowl, and add the fish filets, ensuring each one is coated in pestoPlace a griddle pan onto a high heat Place the pesto-coated fish filets onto the hot griddle pan and grill on both sides until slightly charred, and the fish is cooked through but still juicyServe the fish with the leftover pesto on top

Nutrition: Calories: 488 Protein: 62 g Fat: 25 g Carbs: 1.6 g

White Fish with Chickpeas and Chorizo

Preparation Time: 10 minutes

Cooking Time: 20 minutes

Servings: 4

Ingredients:

2 Tbsp olive oil

4 garlic cloves, finely chopped

1 onion, finely chopped

2 tsp paprika

½ tsp chili powder

5 oz chorizo sausage, sliced

4 large white fresh fish filets

2 cups canned chickpeas (2 cups once drained)

3 large fresh tomatoes, cut into small pieces

Salt and pepper

Fresh coriander/cilantro

Directions:

Place a large sauté pan over a medium-high heat and add the olive oil

Add the garlic and onions to the pan and stir as they soften and become fragrant

Add the paprika, chili, and paprika and stir as the fat in the paprika melts away and the pieces become golden

Shuffle the ingredients in the pan aside to make room for the fish

Add the fish filets to the pan and sprinkle each side with salt and pepper

Cook the fish for about 2 minutes each side until golden

Add the tomatoes and chickpeas to the pan, add more salt and pepper, cover the pan and leave to cook for about 5 minutes

Serve hot, with a generous scattering of coriander/cilantro!

Nutrition: Calories: 460 Protein: 51 g Fat: 19 g

Fresh Salmon with Lemon Butter and New Potatoes

Preparation Time: 10 minutes

Cooking Time: 20 minutes

Servings: 4

Ingredients:

4 filets fresh salmon

2 lemons, thinly sliced

2 Tbsp butter

Salt and pepper

Fresh parsley, finely chopped

1 ½ lbs new potatoes, halved if they are large, just aim for even-sized pieces

Directions:

Preheat the oven to 400 degrees Fahrenheit and line a baking tray with baking paper

Place the salmon onto the tray and rub each fillet with butter, and sprinkle each with salt and pepper

Lay the lemon slices onto each fillet

Slip the tray into the oven and bake until the salmon is just cooked

Meanwhile, prepare the potatoes: place the potatoes in a large saucepan, sprinkle with a generous dose of salt, and cover with water. Cover, and place over a medium-high heat and allow the water to come to a boil. Once the water is boiling, partially remove the lid and allow the potatoes to simmer until soft

Nutrition:

Calories: 428

Protein: 28 g

Fat: 24 g

Carbs: 29 g

Fresh Fish Puttanesca Salad with Couscous

Preparation Time: 10 minutes

Cooking Time: 15 minutes

Servings: 4

Ingredients:

1 cup couscous (uncooked)

1 Tbsp butter

Salt and pepper

2 Tbsp olive oil

1 ½ lbs fresh white fish, cut into even chunks

1 Tbsp dried chili flakes

Salt and pepper

½ cup roughly chopped fresh basil

4 tomatoes, chopped

25 black olives, pits removed, roughly chopped

4 Tbsp capers

Directions:

In a bowl, add the couscous, butter, salt and pepper. Pour over 1 cup of boiling water, cover, and leave as you prepare the rest of the dish

Add the olive oil to a pan over a medium heat

Add the fish and cook on each side until golden and just cooked through

Add the chili pepper and season with salt and pepper, remove from the heat

Use a fork to fluff the couscous and distribute the butter throughout

Divide the couscous between four serving bowls

In a bow, gently combine the fish, basil, tomatoes, olives, and capers

Divide the fish mixture between the four bowl and spoon over the piles of fluffy couscous

Serve with an extra drizzle of olive oil!

Nutrition: Calories: 464 Protein: 40 g Fat: 15 g Carbs: 44 g

Tuna Croquettes

Preparation Time: 40 minutes

Cooking Time: 25 minutes

Servings: 8

Ingredients:

6 tablespoons extra-virgin olive oil, plus 1 to 2 cups

5 tablespoons almond flour, plus 1 cup, divided

1¼ cups heavy cream

1 (4-ounce) can olive oil-packed yellowfin tuna

1 tablespoon chopped red onion

2 teaspoons minced capers

½ teaspoon dried dill

¼ teaspoon freshly ground black pepper

2 large eggs

1 cup panko breadcrumbs (or a gluten-free version)

Directions:

In a large skillet, heat 6 tablespoons olive oil over medium-low heat. Add 5 tablespoons almond flour and cook, stirring constantly, until a smooth paste forms and the flour browns slightly, 2 to 3 minutes.

Increase the heat to medium-high and gradually add the heavy cream, whisking constantly until completely smooth and thickened, another 4 to 5 minutes.

Remove from the heat and stir in the tuna, red onion, capers, dill, and pepper.

Transfer the mixture to an 8-inch square baking dish that is well coated with olive oil and allow to cool to room temperature. Cover and refrigerate until chilled, at least 4 hours or up to overnight.

To form the croquettes, set out three bowls. In one, beat together the eggs. In another, add the remaining almond flour. In the third, add the panko. Line a baking sheet with parchment paper.

Using a spoon, place about a tablespoon of cold prepared dough into the flour mixture and roll to coat. Shake off excess and, using your hands, roll into an oval.

Dip the croquette into the beaten egg, then lightly coat in panko. Set on lined baking sheet and repeat with the remaining dough.

In a small saucepan, heat the remaining 1 to 2 cups of olive oil, so that the oil is about 1 inch deep, over medium-high heat. The smaller the pan, the less oil you will need, but you will need more for each batch.

Test if the oil is ready by throwing a pinch of panko into pot. If it sizzles, the oil is ready for frying. If it sinks, it's not quite ready. Once the oil is heated, fry the croquettes 3 or 4 at a time, depending on the size of your pan, removing with a slotted spoon when golden brown. You will need to adjust the temperature of the oil occasionally to prevent burning. If the croquettes get dark brown very quickly, lower the temperature.

Nutrition:

Calories: 245

Protein: 6 g

Fat: 22 g

Carbs: 7 g

Chapter 13. Dinner Recipes

Stuffed Sardines

Preparation Time: 10 minutes

Cooking Time: 10 minutes

Servings: 6

Ingredients:

¼ c. ricotta cheese

¼ c. shredded Pecorino Romano cheese

¼ c. fresh breadcrumbs

¼ c. chopped parsley

3 large eggs

1 lemon

½ tsp. salt

½ tsp. ground pepper

12 Medium sardines

1/3 c. all-purpose flour

2 c. panko breadcrumbs

1 ½ c. olive oil

Directions:

In a medium bowl combine ricotta, Romano, parsley, fresh breadcrumbs, 1 egg, lemon zest, and ¼ teaspoon of salt and pepper. Once thoroughly combined, set aside.

Next, rinse the sardines and pat them dry with a paper towel. Using the remaining salt and pepper season the inside of each sardine, then stuff each with the ricotta mixture.

Place in three separate dishes place the 2 remaining eggs (lightly beaten), flour, and panko. Then using one hand for wet, and the other for a dry dip each sardine in flour, then egg, then panko. Set sardines down on a plate and set aside.

Start to heat the oil in a large cast-iron skillet, over medium-high heat. You want the oil to be shimmering but not smoking. In batches of 2 fry the sardines in the oil until golden brown, approximately 2-4 minutes for each side. Serve immediately with lemon wedges!

Nutrition: 420 calories 19g carbs 26g protein 26g fat

Mini Greek Meatloaves

Preparation Time: 5 minutes

Cooking Time: 25 minutes

Servings: 6

Ingredients:

Nonstick cooking spray

1 tablespoon extra-virgin olive oil

½ cup minced onion (about ¼ onion)

1 garlic clove, minced (about ½ teaspoon)

1 pound ground beef (93% lean)

½ cup whole-wheat bread crumbs

½ cup crumbled feta cheese (about 2 ounces)

1 large egg

½ teaspoon dried oregano, crushed between your fingers

¼ teaspoon freshly ground black pepper

½ cup 2% plain Greek yogurt

⅓ cup chopped and pitted Kalamata olives

2 tablespoons olive brine

Romaine lettuce or pita bread, for serving (optional)

Directions:

Preheat the oven to 400°F. Coat a 12-cup muffin pan with nonstick cooking spray and set aside.

In a small skillet over medium heat, heat the oil. Add the onion and cook for 4 minutes, stirring frequently. Add the garlic and cook for 1 more minute, stirring frequently. Remove from the heat.

In a large mixing bowl, combine the onion and garlic with the ground beef, bread crumbs, feta, egg, oregano, and pepper. Gently mix together with your hands.

Divide into 12 portions and place in the muffin cups. Cook for 18 to 20 minutes, or until the internal temperature of the meat is 160°F on a meat thermometer. While the meatloaves are baking, in a small bowl, whisk together the yogurt, olives, and olive brine. When you're ready to serve, place the meatloaves on a serving platter and spoon the olive-yogurt sauce on top. You can also serve them on a bed of lettuce or with cut-up pieces of pita bread.

Nutrition: Calories: 244 Total Fat: 13g Saturated Fat: 5g Cholesterol: 87mg Sodium: 355mg Total Carbohydrates: 10g Fiber: 1g Protein: 22g

Yogurt-And-Herb-Marinated Pork Tenderloin

Preparation Time: 6 minutes

Cooking Time: 25 minutes

Servings: 6

Ingredients:

Nonstick cooking spray

2 medium pork tenderloins (10 to 12 ounces each)

½ teaspoon freshly ground black pepper

½ teaspoon kosher or sea salt

¼ cup 2% plain Greek yogurt

1 tablespoon chopped fresh rosemary

Tzatziki yogurt sauce from Chickpea Patties in Pitas (here, step 3) or store-bought tzatziki sauce

1 to 2 tablespoons chopped fresh mint (optional)

Directions:

Preheat the oven to 500°F.

Line a large, rimmed baking sheet with aluminum foil. Place a wire cooling rack on the aluminum foil, and spray the rack with nonstick cooking spray.

Place both pieces of the pork on the wire rack, folding under any skinny ends of the meat to ensure even cooking. Sprinkle both pieces evenly with the pepper and salt.

In a small bowl, mix together the yogurt and rosemary. Using a spoon or your fingers, slather the yogurt mixture over all sides of the pork.

Roast on the wire rack for 10 minutes. Remove the baking sheet from the oven, and turn over both pieces of pork. Roast for 10 to 12 minutes more, or until the internal temperature of the pork measures 145°F on a meat thermometer and the juices run clear. Remove the pork from the rack and place on a clean cutting board. Let rest for 5 minutes, then slice.

While the pork is roasting, make the tzatziki yogurt sauce, adding fresh mint to the sauce, if desired. Serve the sauce with the pork.

Nutrition: Calories: 183 Total Fat: 10g Saturated Fat: 3g Cholesterol: 73mg Sodium: 372mg Total Carbohydrates: 4g Fiber: 0g Protein: 22g

Rosemary Potatoes

Preparation Time: 10 minutes

Cooking Time: 20 minutes

Servings: 6

Ingredients:

2 lbs baby potatoes

1 fresh rosemary sprig

1 cup vegetable stock

1/4 cup olive oil - 2 garlic cloves

Pepper

Salt

Directions: Add oil into the inner pot of instant pot and set the pot on sauté mode. Add garlic, potatoes, and rosemary and cook for 10 minutes. Add stock, pepper, and salt and stir well. Seal pot with lid and cook on high for 10 minutes. Once done, release pressure using quick release. Remove lid. Serve and enjoy.

Nutrition: Calories 163 Fat 8.6 g Carbohydrates 19.4 g Sugar 0.1 g Protein 4 g Cholesterol 0 mg

Delicious Italian Bell Pepper

Preparation Time: 10 minutes

Cooking Time: 13 minutes

Servings: 4

Ingredients:

5 bell peppers, cut into strips

2 tbsp fresh parsley, chopped

1 tbsp garlic, chopped

2 tomatoes, chopped

1 onion, sliced

1 tbsp olive oil

Pepper

Salt

Directions:

Add oil into the inner pot of instant pot and set the pot on sauté mode.

Add onion and sauté for 3 minutes.

Add garlic and bell peppers and cook for 5 minutes.

Add remaining ingredients and stir well.

Seal pot with lid and cook on high for 5 minutes.

Once done, release pressure using quick release. Remove lid.

Stir well and serve.

Nutrition: Calories 103 Fat 4.1 g

Carbohydrates 17 g Sugar 10.3 g Protein 2.5 g Cholesterol 0 mg

Pesto Zucchini

Preparation Time: 10 minutes

Cooking Time: 8 minutes

Servings: 4

Ingredients:

2 zucchinis, sliced

1 cup vegetable stock

1 tsp Italian seasoning

2 tbsp olive oil

1 cup mozzarella cheese, shredded

1 eggplant, sliced

1 bell pepper, cut into strips

1/4 cup basil pesto

Pepper

Salt

Directions:

Add all ingredients except pesto into the instant pot and stir well.

Seal pot with lid and cook on high for 8 minutes.

Once done, release pressure using quick release. Remove lid.

Stir well. Top with basil pesto and serve.

Nutrition:

Calories 139

Fat 9.1 g

Carbohydrates 12.9 g

Sugar 6.9 g Protein 4.8 g Cholesterol 5 mg

Pesto Cauliflower

Preparation Time: 10 minutes

Cooking Time: 8 minutes

Servings: 2

Ingredients:

2 cups cauliflower florets

1 tbsp olive oil

1 tbsp fresh lemon juice

1/4 cup pine nuts

2 tbsp cream cheese

1/2 cup spinach, chopped

1 avocado, sliced

1/2 tsp red pepper flakes

1/4 tsp dried mint

1/4 tsp dried thyme

1/4 tsp dried rosemary

1 tsp sea salt

Directions:

Add cauliflower into the instant pot. Add water to cover the cauliflower.

Seal pot with lid and cook on high for 5 minutes.

Once done, release pressure using quick release. Remove lid.

Drain cauliflower well and set aside. Clean the instant pot.

Add avocado, spinach, cream cheese, pine nuts, lemon juice, rosemary, thyme, mint, and salt into the blender and blend until smooth.

Add oil into the inner pot of instant pot and set the pot on sauté mode.

Add cauliflower and blended avocado mixture into the pot and stir well and cook for 2 minutes.

Serve and enjoy.

Nutrition:

Calories 445

Fat 42 g Carbohydrates 17.3 g Sugar 3.8 g

Protein 7.3 g

Cholesterol 11 mg

Italian Tomato Mushrooms

Preparation Time: 10 minutes

Cooking Time: 13 minutes

Servings: 2

Ingredients:

1 cup tomatoes, chopped

2 cups mushrooms, sliced

1 tbsp olive oil

1/2 cup zucchini, chopped

1/4 cup green onions, chopped

1 cup cream cheese

1/2 tsp mint, chopped

1/2 tsp dried rosemary

1/2 tsp dried oregano

Salt

Directions:

Add tomatoes, rosemary, oregano, mint, and salt into the blender and blend until smooth.

Add oil into the inner pot of instant pot and set the pot on sauté mode.

Add green onion and zucchini and sauté for 5 minutes. Transfer zucchini and onion mixture on a plate.

Add 1 cup water and mushrooms into the pot and stir well.

Seal pot with lid and cook on high for 3 minutes.

Once done, release pressure using quick release. Remove lid.

Add blended tomato mixture, zucchini, and cream cheese and cook on sauté mode for 5 minutes.

Stir well and serve.

Nutrition:

Calories 507

Fat 48 g

Carbohydrates 11.2 g

Sugar 4.6 g

Protein 12.4 g Cholesterol 128 mg

Chickpea & Potato

Preparation Time: 10 minutes

Cooking Time: 8 minutes

Servings: 2

Ingredients:

1 cup cooked chickpeas

1/2 tsp ground cumin

1 tsp ground coriander

1/4 tsp ginger

2 potatoes, peeled and cubed

1 cup tomatoes, diced

1 onion, chopped

1 tbsp olive oil

1/4 cup vegetable stock

1 tsp turmeric

1/2 tsp salt

Directions:

Add oil into the inner pot of instant pot and set the pot on sauté mode.

Add onion and potatoes and cook for 2-3 minutes.

Add remaining ingredients and stir everything well.

Seal pot with lid and cook on high for 5 minutes.

Once done, allow to release pressure naturally for 10 minutes then release remaining using quick release. Remove lid.

Serve and enjoy.

Nutrition:

Calories 617

Fat 13.7 g

Carbohydrates 104 g

Sugar 18 g

Protein 24.5 g

Cholesterol 0 mg

Zesty Green Beans

Preparation Time: 10 minutes

Cooking Time: 15 minutes

Servings: 4

Ingredients:

1 lb green beans, trimmed

1 cup vegetable stock

1 lemon juice

1 tsp lemon zest, grated

Pepper

Salt

Directions:

Pour the stock into the instant pot.

Add green beans, lemon juice, lemon zest, pepper, and salt into the bowl and toss well.

Transfer green beans into the steamer basket. Place a steamer basket in the pot.

Seal pot with lid and cook on high for 15 minutes.

Once done, allow to release pressure naturally for 5 minutes then release remaining using quick release. Remove lid.

Serve and enjoy.

Nutrition: Calories 40 Fat 0.3 g Carbohydrates 8.7 g

Sugar 2.1 g Protein 2.3 g Cholesterol 0 mg

Walnut-Rosemary Crusted Salmon

Preparation Time: 10 minutes

Cooking Time: 20 minutes

Servings: 4

Ingredients:

2 teaspoons of Dijon mustard

1 minced clove garlic

¼ teaspoon of lemon zest

½ teaspoon of honey

½ teaspoon of kosher salt

1 teaspoon of chopped fresh rosemary

3 tablespoons of panko breadcrumbs

¼ teaspoon of crushed red pepper

3 tablespoons of finely chopped walnuts

1 pound of frozen or fresh skinless salmon fillet

1 teaspoon of extra-virgin olive oil

Olive oil

Directions:

Preheat the oven to 420°F and use parchment paper to line a rimmed baking sheet.

Combine mustard, lemon zest, garlic, lemon juice, honey, rosemary, crushed red pepper, and salt in a bowl.

Combine walnuts and panko, with oil, in another bowl.

Place the salmon on that baking sheet. Spread that mustard mix on the fish, along with the panko mix. Make sure the fish is adequately coated with the mixtures. Spray olive oil lightly on the salmon.

Bake for about 8-12 minutes (till the salmon can be separated using a fork).

Nutrition:

Carbohydrate – 4 g

Protein – 24 g

Fat – 12 g Calories: 222 calories

Caprese Stuffed Portobello Mushrooms

Preparation Time: 25 minutes

Cooking Time: 40 minutes

Servings: 2

Ingredients:

3 tablespoons of divided extra-virgin olive oil

1 medium minced clove garlic

½ teaspoon of salt

½ teaspoon of ground pepper

About 14 ounces of Portobello mushrooms, with gills and stems, removed

1 cup of halved cherry tomatoes

A ½ cup of fresh and drained mozzarella pearls patted dry

A ½ cup of thinly sliced fresh basil

2 teaspoons of balsamic vinegar

Directions:

Preheat the oven to 400°F. Combine a ¼ teaspoon of salt, two tablespoons of oil, and a ¼ teaspoon of pepper in a bowl. Use a brush for coating the mushrooms with this mixture.

Place the mushrooms on a baking sheet and bake it for about ten minutes (till the mushrooms get soft).

Stir basil, tomatoes, and mozzarella in a pan. Mix 1 tablespoon of oil, a ¼ teaspoon of salt, and a ¼ teaspoon of pepper in a bowl.

Remove the components of the pan after the mushrooms soften. Fill the mushrooms with the tomato mix.

Bake till the tomatoes wilt and the cheese melts, for about 15 minutes. Drizzle the mushrooms with half teaspoons of vinegar before serving.

Nutrition:

Carbohydrate – 6 g

Protein – 6 g

Fat – 16 g

Calories: 186 calories

Greek Salad Nachos

Preparation Time: 15 minutes

Cooking Time: 15 minutes

Servings: 6

Ingredients:

A ⅓ cup of hummus

2 tablespoons of extra-virgin olive oil

1 tablespoon of lemon juice

¼ teaspoon of ground pepper

3 cups of whole-grain pita chips

1 cup of chopped lettuce

A ½ cup of quartered grape tomatoes

A ¼ cup of crumbled feta cheese

2 tablespoons of chopped olives

2 tablespoons of minced red onion

1 tablespoon of minced fresh oregano

Directions:

Whisk pepper, lemon juice, oil, and hummus in a bowl.

Spread the pita chips on a plate in one layer.

Cover the chips with about ¾ of that hummus mix and top it with tomatoes, red onion, olives, feta, and lettuce. Cover it with the rest of the hummus. Sprinkle oregano on top before serving it.

Nutrition:

Carbohydrate – 13 g

Protein – 4 g

Fat – 10 g Calories: 159 calories

Greek Chicken with Lemon Vinaigrette and Roasted Spring Vegetables

Preparation Time: 30 minutes

Cooking Time: 50 minutes

Servings: 4

Ingredients:

For the lemon vinaigrette

1 lemon

1 tablespoon olive oil

1 tablespoon crumbled feta cheese

½ teaspoon honey

For the Greek Chicken and roasted veggies

8 ounce of boneless, skinless chicken breast, cut lengthwise in half

A ¼ cup of light mayonnaise

6 cloves of minced garlic

A ½ cup of panko bread crumbs

3 tablespoons of grated Parmesan cheese

½ teaspoon of kosher salt

½ teaspoon of black pepper

1-inch pieces of asparagus, 2 cups

1½ cups of sliced cremini mushrooms

1½ cups of halved cherry tomatoes

1 tablespoon of olive oil

Directions:

To make the vinaigrette, put half teaspoons of zest, one tablespoon of lemon juice, olive oil, cheese, and honey in a bowl.

For the vegetables and chicken, preheat the oven to 470°F. Use a meat mallet for flattening the chicken between two pieces of plastic wrap.

Place the chicken in a bowl and add two garlic cloves and mayonnaise. Mix cheese, bread crumbs, a ¼ teaspoon of pepper, and a ¼ teaspoon of salt together. Dip the chicken in this crumb mix. Spray olive oil over the chicken.

Roast in the oven till the chicken is done and vegetables are tender. Sprinkle dill over it and serve.

Nutrition:

Carbohydrate – 12 g

Protein – 29 g

Fat – 15 g

Calories: 306 calories

Chicken in Tomato-Balsamic Pan Sauce

Preparation Time: 35 minutes

Cooking Time: 35 minutes

Servings: 4

Ingredients:

2 8-ounce skinless, boneless chicken breasts

½ teaspoon of salt

½ teaspoon of ground pepper

A ¼ cup of white whole-wheat flour

3 tablespoons of extra-virgin olive oil

A ½ cup of halved cherry tomatoes

2 tablespoons of sliced shallot

A ¼ cup of balsamic vinegar

1 cup of low-sodium chicken broth

1 tablespoon of minced garlic

1 tablespoon of toasted and crushed fennel seeds

1 tablespoon of butter

Directions:

Slice the chicken breasts into 4 pieces and beat them with a mallet till it reaches a thickness of a ¼ inch. Use ¼ teaspoons of pepper and salt to coat the chicken.

Heat two tablespoons of oil in a skillet and keep the heat to a medium. Cook the chicken breasts for two minutes on each side. Transfer it to a serving plate and cover it with foil to keep it warm.

Add one tablespoon oil, shallot, and tomatoes in a pan and cook till it softens. Add vinegar and boil the mix till the vinegar gets reduced by half. Put fennel seeds, garlic, salt, and pepper and cook for about four minutes. Remove it from the heat and stir it with butter.

Pour this sauce over chicken and serve.

Nutrition: Carbohydrate – 9 g Protein – 25 g Fat – 17 g Calories: 294 calories

Chicken Souvlaki Kebabs with Mediterranean Couscous

Preparation Time: 45 minutes

Cooking Time: 2 hours and 20 minutes

Servings: 4

Ingredients:

For the Kebabs-

1 pound of boneless, skinless chicken breast halves in ½-inch strips

1 cup of sliced fennel

⅓ Cup of dry white wine

A ¼ cup of lemon juice

3 tablespoons of canola oil

4 cloves of garlic, minced

2 teaspoons dried and crushed oregano

½ teaspoon salt

¼ teaspoon black pepper

Couscous-

1 teaspoon of olive oil

A ½ cup of Israeli couscous

1 cup of water

A ½ cup of snipped dried tomatoes

A ¾ cup of chopped red sweet pepper

½ cup each of chopped cucumber and red onion

⅓ Cup of plain fat-free Greek yogurt

A ¼ cup of fresh basil leaves, thinly sliced

A ¼ cup of snipped fresh parsley

1 tablespoon of lemon juice

¼ teaspoon of salt

¼ teaspoon of black pepper

Directions:

Place chicken with sliced fennel in a sealable plastic bag and set aside. Combine the lemon juice, white wine, oil, oregano, garlic, pepper, and salt in a bowl for the marinade. Take a ¼ cup of this marinade and set aside.

Pour rest of the marinade over the chicken and refrigerate for 1 ½ hour.

Take wooden skewers and thread chicken on to it in accordion style.

Grill the chicken skewers for six to eight minutes.

Put all the ingredients of couscous in a pan and cook it in olive oil. Serve it alongside the chicken.

Nutrition:

Carbohydrate – 28 g

Protein – 32 g

Fat – 9 g

Calories: 322 calories

Caprese Chicken Hasselback style

Preparation Time: 25 minutes

Cooking Time: 50 minutes

Servings: 4

Ingredients:

2 skinless, boneless chicken breasts - 8 ounces each

½ teaspoon of salt

½ teaspoon of ground pepper

1 medium tomato, sliced

3 ounces of fresh mozzarella, halved and sliced

A ¼ cup of prepared pesto

8 cups of broccoli florets

2 tablespoons of olive oil

Directions:

Preheat the oven to 375°F and coat a rimmed baking sheet with cooking spray.

Make crosswire cuts at half inches in the chicken breasts. Sprinkle pepper and salt on them. Fill the cuts with mozzarella slices and tomato alternatively. Brush both the chicken breasts with pesto and put it on the baking sheet.

Mix broccoli, oil, salt, and pepper in a bowl. Put in the tomatoes if there are any left. Put this mixture on one side of the baking sheet.

Bake till the broccoli is tender, and the chicken is not pink in the center. Cut each of the breasts in half and serve.

Nutrition: Carbohydrate – 10 g Protein – 38 g Fat – 19 g Calories: 355 calories

Simple Grilled Salmon with Veggies

Preparation Time: 25 minutes

Cooking Time: 25 minutes

Servings: 4

Ingredients:

1 medium zucchini, lengthwise halved

2 orange, red or yellow bell peppers, halved, trimmed, and seeded

1 medium red onion, cut into wedges of 1-inch

1 tablespoon of olive oil

½ teaspoon salt and ground pepper

1¼ pounds salmon fillet, cut into 4 pieces

¼ cup thinly sliced fresh basil

1 lemon, cut into 4 wedges

Directions:

Preheat the grill to medium-high. Brush peppers, zucchini, and onion with oil. Sprinkle a ¼ teaspoon of salt over it. Sprinkle salmon with salt and pepper.

Place the veggies and the salmon on the grill. Cook the veggies for six to eight minutes on each side, till the grill marks appear. Cook the salmon till it flakes when you test it with a fork.

When cooled down, chop the veggies roughly and mix it together in a bowl. You can remove the salmon skin to serve with the veggies. Each serving can be garnished with a tablespoon of basil and a lemon wedge.

Nutrition: Carbohydrate – 6 g Protein – 6 g Fat – 16 g Calories: 186 calories

Greek Turkey Burgers with Spinach, Feta &Tzatziki

Preparation Time: 30 minutes

Cooking Time: 30 minutes

Servings: 4

Ingredients:

One cup of chopped spinach, frozen and thawed

One pound of lean 93% turkey, ground

Half cup of feta cheese, crumbled

Half tsp. of garlic powder

Half tsp. of oregano, dried

One-fourth tsp. of salt

One-fourth tsp. of pepper, ground

Four hamburger buns, small and whole-wheat

Four tsp. of tzatziki

Twelve slices of cucumber

Eight red onion, thick rings

Directions:

Pre-heat the grill to med-high.

Squeeze moisture from spinach and combine it with turkey, garlic powder, feta, pepper, and salt in a bowl to mix well.

Form 4 four inches of patties and oil the grill rack.

Until cooked, grill patties for four to six minutes for each side until the thermometer reads 165°F.

Assemble burgers on buns and top each with 1 tsp. of tzatziki, two onion rings, and three cucumbers.

Wrap them and refrigerate for eight hours.

Nutrition: Carbohydrate – 28 g Protein – 30 g Fat – 17 g Calories: 376 calories

Mediterranean Chicken Quinoa Bowl

Preparation Time: 30 minutes

Cooking Time: 30 minutes

Servings: 4

Ingredients:

One pound of skinless and boneless trimmed chicken breasts

One-fourth tsp. of salt

One-fourth tsp. of pepper, ground

1 seven-ounce jar of red pepper, rinsed and roasted

One-fourth cup of almonds, slivered

Four tsps. of olive oil, extra-virgin and divided

Half tsp. of cumin, ground

One-fourth tsp. of red pepper, crushed

Two cups of quinoa, cooked

One-fourth cup of Kalamata olives, pitted and chopped

One-fourth cup of red onion, finely chopped

One cup of cucumber, diced

One-fourth cup of feta cheese, crumbled

Two tsp. of fresh parsley, finely chopped

Directions:

Place a rack in the oven and preheat to lime rimmed baking sheet along with foil

Sprinkle the chicken with pepper and salt to place on the baking sheet. Broil until the thermometer reads 165°F. Then transfer chicken to a cutting board.

Place almonds, oil, pepper, cumin, red pepper, paprika together and puree it.

Combine olives, quinoa, red onion, and the remaining two tablespoons of oil in a bowl.

Before serving, sprinkle the dish with parsley and feta.

Nutrition: Carbohydrate – 31 g Protein – 34 g Fat – 27 g Calories: 519 calories

Creamy Dill Potatoes

Preparation Time: 10 minutes

Cooking Time: 20 minutes

Servings: 4

Ingredients:

2 lbs potatoes, peeled and cut into chunks

1 tbsp fresh dill, chopped

1 cup vegetable stock

3/4 cup heavy cream

Pepper

Salt

Directions:

Add all ingredients into the inner pot of instant pot and stir well.

Seal pot with lid and cook on high for 20 minutes.

Once done, allow to release pressure naturally for 10 minutes then release remaining using quick release. Remove lid.

Stir and serve.

Nutrition:

Calories 238

Fat 8.6 g

Carbohydrates 37 g Sugar 2.8 g Protein 4.5 g Cholesterol 31 mg

Chapter 14. Snacks Recipes

Mediterranean Flatbread with Toppings

Preparation Time: 10 minutes

Cooking Time: 15 minutes

Servings: 10

Ingredients:

2 medium tomatoes

5 black olives (diced)

8 ounces of crescent rolls

1 clove of garlic (finely chopped)

1 red onion (sliced)

¼ tbs. salt

4 tbs. olive oil

¼ tbs. pepper powder

1 and ½ tbs. Italian seasoning

Parmesan cheese as per requirement

Directions:

Wash and clean the tomatoes properly. Then make very thin and round slices with a sharp knife. You have to ensure that the tomato juices drain out. So, place these on a dry piece of linen cloth.

You will get crescent rolls or flatbread dough in the market. Unroll these and keep these on a big baking tray. Make sure the surface of the baking dish has no grease or water.

Then roll the dough into several portions, which will not be more than 14x10 inches in measurement.

With the help of a rolling pin, shape these into rectangular flatbreads.

Place the tomato slices, diced black olive and onion slices on these flatbreads.

Add the Italian seasoning, olive oil, pepper powder, salt, and chopped garlic together and mix well.

Take the mixture and apply an even coat on all the flatbreads. This mixture will add flavor to the toppings and flatbreads.

Put the baking tray in the microwave oven and set the temperature at 375°.

After 15 minutes, remove the plate from the oven and enjoy your crunchy Mediterranean flatbread with toppings with a glass of red wine.

Nutrition:

Carbohydrate – 9g

Protein - 2g Fat – 6g Calories: 101

Smoked Salmon and Goat Cheese Bites

Preparation Time: 10 minutes

Cooking Time: 15 minutes

Servings: 12

Ingredients:

8 ounces of goat cheese

1 tbs. of fresh rosemary

2 tbs. of oregano

2 tbs. of basil (fresh)

2 cloves of garlic (chopped)

4 ounces fresh smoked salmon

½ tbs. salt

½ tbs pepper

Directions:

People, living in the Mediterranean regions love to eat fish, especially fatty fish like salmon. This is a classic Mediterranean diet snack that combines the smoky flavors of salmon and the sweet and tanginess of goat cheese.

Put the three herbs on the chopping board and run a knife vigorously through these. Once the herbs have been mixed well, transfer it to a medium sized bowl

The add goat cheese (grated), chopped garlic, pepper and salt in the bowl and mix properly. Keep this mixture for some time to rest.

There are two ways of serving salmon-goat cheese bites. Either you can place a flat piece of smoked salmon on the tray and top it with a dollop of goat cheese and seasoning mix.

The other way is to make small balls with the goat cheese and seasoning mix and wrap a wide stripe of smoked salmon around the ball.

One can also sprinkle some additional Italian seasoning on the final salmon bites to enhance the taste. This step is optional, and omitting it will not mar the original richness of the salmon-cheese bites.

Nutrition: Carbohydrate – 17.33g   Protein - 54.83g   Fat – 53.33g Calories: 739

Mediterranean Chickpea Bowl

Preparation Time: 12 minutes

Cooking Time: 13 minutes

Servings: 2Ingredients:

½ tbs. of cumin seeds

1 large julienned carrot

A ¼ cup of tomatoes (chopped)

1 medium julienned zucchini

A ¼ cup of lemon juice

2 sliced green chilies

¼ cup of olive oil

A ½ cup of chopped parsley leaves

1 minced clove of garlic

¼ tbs. salt

¼ tbs. cayenne pepper powder

A ¼ cup of radish (sliced)

3 tbs. walnuts (chopped)

1/3 feta cheese (crumbled)

1 big can of chickpeas

Proportionate salad greens

Directions:

Another ingredient that you will see on the Mediterranean Diet list is chickpeas. The Mediterranean Chickpea Bowl is a popular snack that can be enjoyed at all times. You can use fresh or canned chickpeas as per preference.

For the salad, you will have to make a special dressing that will make the dish tasty. You need to roast the cumin seeds on a dry pan. Make sure the heat is at medium.

When the seeds begin releasing the aroma, put the seeds in a different mixing bowl.

In this bowl, add the olive oil, garlic, lemon juice, and tomatoes. Also, add the cayenne pepper and salt, and mix well to blend in all the ingredients.

Take a big bowl and add the chickpeas into it. Then put in the sliced and chopped veggies, and parsley leaves.

Adding walnut pieces will add an extra crunch to the Mediterranean chickpea salad.

Put in the seasoning you just prepared and then, mix all the ingredients well.

Nutrition:

Carbohydrate – 30g

Protein - 12g

Fat – 38g

Calories: 492

Hummus Snack Bowl

Preparation Time: 5 minutes

Cooking Time: 5 minutes

Servings: 2

Ingredients:

8 tbs of hummus

½ cup fresh spinach (coarsely chopped)

½ cups of carrots (shredded)

1 big tomato (diced)

¼ tbs. salt

¼ tbs. chili powder

¼ tbs. pepper

6 sweet olives (3 green, 3 black, chopped)

Directions:

The Mediterranean Diet will not be complete without the use of hummus. They don't indulge in fast food, but opt for fresh salad bowls, which are full of nutrition and goodness.

You can either prepare the hummus at home or purchase a jar that does not contain added flavorings and preservatives.

Take a large bowl and put in 6 spoonfuls of hummus into it. In this, put in chopped olives, shredded carrots, spinach leaves, and diced tomatoes.

Coat these vegetables with hummus properly.

After mixing the vegetables and hummus paste for at least five minutes, add in the chili powder. Make sure that it is evenly spread into the whole salad.

Lastly, add pepper powder and salt in the hummus-veggies mixture. You can taste the mixture and check the balance of all the ingredients.

Some also drizzle on some extra virgin olive oil onto the salad. This step is optional and can be omitted.

The Hummus Snack Bowl is a complete snack on its own. If you desire to add some texture to it, some freshly baked flatbreads or bread will complement the salad.

Nutrition:

Carbohydrate – 43g

Protein – 12g

Fat – 10g

Calories: 280

Crock-Pot Paleo Chunky Mix

Preparation Time: 5 minutes

Cooking Time: 1 hour and 30 minutes

Servings: 2

Ingredients:

4 cups of walnuts (raw and roughly broken)

2 cups of cashews (raw and broken in halves)

2 cups of plain coconut flakes

2/3 cups of sugar granules

2 tbs. of olive oil of fresh butter

2 tbs. of extracts of vanilla

12 ounces of dry banana chips

1 and ½ cups of dark chocolate (broken in chips)

Directions:

As the people of the Mediterranean region love to eat nuts, this is one snack that you will find in each household. It is full of good fats and gives you energy and healthy bones. The preparation is rather simple, but the cooking process is lengthy.

To prepare this dish, you will require a medium-sized crock pot.

In this pot, pour in the pieces of walnut, vanilla essence, sugar granules, and olive oil.

After this, you must mix the ingredients well and place the pot on high heat.

Leave the pot at high temperature for around 60 minutes.

After one hour, you need to reduce the heat to low and cook the mixture for another half an hour.

Once the 30 minutes are over, empty the contents of this pot on a dry piece of parchment sheet.

After resting the mix for 15 minutes, you need to put the chocolate chips and banana chips.

Then mix all these ingredients together. The addition of chocolate will add richness to the sweet and nutty snack.

Nutrition:

Carbohydrate – 18.6g

Protein – 4g

Fat – 7g

Calories: 250

Smoked Eggplant Dip

Preparation Time: 20 minutes

Cooking Time: 40 minutes

Servings: 4

Ingredients:

1 and a ½ pound of eggplant

½ tbsp. pepper powder

1 medium coarsely chopped onion

4 tbs. of olive oil

6 peeled cloves of garlic

2 cups of sour cream

¾ tbs. salt

4 tbs. of lemon juice

Fresh parsley (minced)

Liquid smoke (10 drops; optional)

Directions:

Salads, dressing, and dips are predominant in the Mediterranean diet. But not many are aware that eggplant can be used to make a mean dip that will you change the way you view this versatile vegetable.

To start with, you need to peel the outer skin of the eggplants. Using a peeler will come in handy for this task.

As a significant part of the cooking will be done in the oven, it is best to preheat it. Crank up the temperature to 400 degrees.

Make 1-inch thick slices of the eggplant. It will ensure the penetration of flavors and even cooking.

Take an oven baking tray and brush some olive oil onto the pan. Place the eggplant slices on the pan in an orderly fashion.

Sprinkle a thick layer of chopped onions on the eggplant slices. On that, place the cloves of garlic.

Roast the veggies inside the oven for 45 minutes. It is best to bring out the tray once and toss the ingredients.

Once the slices are evenly cooked and cooled, it is time to make a paste in the blender.

When you are happy with the texture of the mixture, add the lemon juice and sour cream into it.

After mixing all the ingredients, put in pepper powder and salt. Adding liquid smoke is optional.

After sprinkling in minced fresh parsley leaves, the dip is ready to be consumed with flatbread or banana chips.

Nutrition: Carbohydrate – 5g Protein - 3g Fat – 5g Calories: 77

Savory Spinach Feta and Sweet Pepper Muffins

Preparation Time: 10 minutes

Cooking Time: 25 minutes

Servings: 10

Ingredients:

2 and ½ cups of flour

2 tbs. of baking powder

A ¼ cup of sugar

¾ tbs. salt

1 tbs. paprika

A ¾ cup of milk

2 fresh eggs

½ cup olive oil

A ¾ cup of feta (crumbled)

1 and ¼ cups of sliced spinach

1/3 cup of Florina peppers

Directions:

If you are looking for a Mediterranean diet snack that will not only fill your belly but will create an explosion of tastes in your mouth, then this is the ultimate option.

As the muffins will be baked in the oven, you need to preheat it to a temperature of 190 degrees.

Take a deep and large container. In this, put in the sugar, baking powder, salt, and flour. Mix all these dry ingredients properly and make sure there are no lumps.

In a separate container, you need to pour in the milk, eggs and the olive oil. Stir these ingredients so that they form one smooth liquid.

Carefully pour in the liquids in the container that has the dry ingredients. Use your hand to mix everything well, so that a thick and smooth dough is formed.

Then it is time to put in the crumbled feta, pepper and sliced spinach into the dough. Then spend some time with it to ensure that the new ingredients have mixed evenly into the muffin dough.

You can get muffin trays at the market. In such a tray, scoop out portions of the dough and place it into the muffin tray depressions.

Put in this pan inside the oven for 25 minutes. After cooling, the muffins will be ready for consumption.

Nutrition:

Carbohydrate – 15g

Protein – 10g

Fat – 20g

Calories: 240

Italian Oven Roasted Vegetables

Preparation Time: 5 minutes

Cooking Time: 30 minutes

Servings: 4

Ingredients:

2 sliced medium onions

½ tbs. salt

1 tbs. Italian seasoning

2 sliced yellow squash

1/8 tsp pepper powder

3 minced cloves of garlic

2 sweet and large green and red peppers

2 tbs. olive oil

Directions:

Salads form a big part of the Mediterranean diet. The secret to the health and well-being of these people is due to their high vegetable and fruit consumption. If you want to acquire the healthy inner glow, then sacking on these roasted Italian salads will come in handy.

Mixing is an art, and the taste of the salad will depend on how well you mix the ingredients.

Take all the cut, chopped, minced and diced vegetables and put them in a large salad mixing bowl.

After this, you will have to add required amounts of salt, Italian seasoning and pepper powder in the vegetables.

Toss these ingredients for some time to ensure that everything has mixed well.

Then pour in the olive oil into this mixture and again blend well.

Place the marinated vegetables in a roasting oven and put it inside the microwave oven.

The oven must be preheated at 425-degree temperature. The baking will take no longer than 25 minutes.

After pulling out the tray from the oven, you can sprinkle on some extra cheese. This is optional and can be omitted.

Nutrition:

Carbohydrate – 16g

Protein - 3g

Fat – 4g

Calories: 100

Greek Spinach Yogurt Artichoke Dip

Preparation Time: 10 minutes

Cooking Time: 10 minutes

Servings: 2

Ingredients:

1 tbs. olive oil

9-ounces spinach (roughly chopped)

¼ cup Parmesan cheese (grated)

14 ounces Artichoke hearts (chopped)

½ tbsp. pepper powder - ½ tbs. onion powder

½ tbs. garlic powder - 8 ounces sliced chestnuts

2 cups of Greek yogurt (fat-free)

Directions:

Preheat the oven to 350°F. Chop artichoke hearts into bite-sized pieces. Mix all ingredients together and season with a pinch of salt; pour into a small casserole or oven-safe dish (about 1-quart). Sprinkle the top with extra mozzarella cheese. Bake for 20-22 minutes, or until heated through and the cheese on top is melted. Serve warm with pita or tortilla chips.

Nutrition: Carbohydrate – 20.9 g Protein - 16.3 g Fat – 2.9 g Calories: 170

Sautéed Apricots

Preparation Time: 5 minutes

Cooking Time: 15 Minutes

Servings: 4

Ingredients:

2 Tablespoons Olive Oil

1 Cup Almonds, Blanched, Skinless & Unsalted

½ Teaspoon Sea Salt, Fine

1/8 Teaspoon Red Pepper Flakes

1/8 Teaspoon Cinnamon, Ground

½ Cup Apricots, Dried & Chopped

Directions:

Place a frying pan over high heat, adding in your almonds, salt and olive oil. Sauté until the almonds turn a light gold, which will take five to ten minutes. Make sure to stir often because they burn easily.

Spoon your almonds into a serving dish, adding in your cinnamon, red pepper flakes, and chopped apricot.

Allow it to cool before serving.

Nutrition:

Calories: 207 Protein: 5 Grams Fat: 19 Grams Carbs: 7 Grams

Spiced Kale Chips

Preparation Time: 5 minutes

Cooking Time: 35 Minutes

Servings: 4

Ingredients:

1 Tablespoon Olive Oil

½ Teaspoon Chili Powder

¼ Teaspoon Sea Salt, Fine

3 Cups Kale, Stemmed, Washed & Torn into 2 Inch Pieces

Directions:

Start by heating your oven to 300, and then get out two baking sheets. Line each baking sheet with parchment paper before placing them to the side.

Dry your kale off completely before placing it in a bowl, and add in your olive oil. Make sure the kale is thoroughly coated before seasoning it.

Spread your kale out on your baking sheets in a single layer, baking for twenty-five minutes. Your kale will need roasted halfway through, and it should turn out dry and crispy. Allow them to cool for at least five minutes before serving.

Nutrition: Calories: 56 Protein: 2 Grams Fat: 4 Grams Carbs: 5 Grams

Yogurt Dip

Preparation Time: 5 minutes

Cooking Time: 10 Minutes

Servings: 4

Ingredients:

½ Lemon, Juiced & Zested

1 Cup Greek Yogurt, Plain

1 Tablespoon Chives, Fresh & Chopped Fine

2 Teaspoons Dill, Fresh & Chopped

2 Teaspoons Thyme, Fresh & Chopped

1 Teaspoon Parsley, Fresh & Chopped

½ Teaspoon Garlic, Minced

¼ Teaspoon Sea Salt, Fine

Directions:

Get out a bowl and mix all of your ingredients together until they're well blended. Season with salt before refrigerating. Serve chilled.

Nutrition:

Calories: 59

Protein: 2 Grams Fat: 4 Grams Carbs: 5 Grams

Zucchini Fritters

Preparation Time: 5 minutes

Cooking Time: 30 Minutes

Servings: 6

Ingredients:

2 Zucchinis, Peeled & Grated

1 Sweet Onion, Diced Fine

2 Cloves Garlic, Minced

1 Cup Parsley, Fresh & Chopped

½ Teaspoon Sea Salt, Fine

½ Teaspoon Black Pepper

½ Teaspoon Allspice, Ground

2 Tablespoons Olive Oil

4 Eggs, Large

Directions:

Get out a plate and line it with paper towels before setting it to the side.

Get out a large bowl and mix your onion, parsley, garlic, zucchini, pepper, allspice and sea salt together.

Get out a different bowl and beat your eggs before adding them to your zucchini mixture. Make sure it's mixed well.

Get out a large skillet and place it over medium heat. Heat up your olive oil, and then scoop ¼ cup at a time into the skillet to create your fritters. Cook for three minutes or until the bottom sets. Flip and cook for an additional three minutes. Transfer them to your plate so they can drain. Serve with pita bread or on their own.

Nutrition:

Calories: 103

Protein: 5 Grams

Fat: 8 Grams

Carbs: 5 Grams

Easy Hummus

Preparation Time: 5 minutes

Cooking Time: 5 Minutes

Servings: 6

Ingredients:

3 Cloves Garlic, Crushed

1 Tablespoon Olive Oil

1 Teaspoon Sea Salt, Fine

16 Ounces Canned Garbanzo Beans, Drained

1 ½ Tablespoons Tahini

½ Cup Lemon Juice, Fresh

Directions:

Blend your garbanzo beans, tahini, garlic, olive oil, lemon juice and sea salt together for three to five minutes in a blender. Make sure it's mixed well. It should be fluffy and soft.

Refrigerate for at least an hour before serving with either pita bread or cut vegetables.

Nutrition:

Calories: 187

Protein: 8 Gram

Fat: 7 Grams

Carbs: 25 Grams

Cucumber Bites

Preparation time: 10 minutes

Cooking time: 0 minutes

Servings: 12

Ingredients:

1 English cucumber, sliced into 32 rounds

10 ounces hummus

16 cherry tomatoes, halved

1 tablespoon parsley, chopped

1 ounce feta cheese, crumbled

Directions:

Spread the hummus on each cucumber round, divide the tomato halves on each, sprinkle the cheese and parsley on to and serve as an appetizer.

Nutrition: calories 162, fat 3.4, fiber 2, carbs 6.4, protein 2.4

Stuffed Avocado

Preparation time: 10 minutes

Cooking time: 0 minutes

Servings: 2

Ingredients:

1 avocado, halved and pitted

10 ounces canned tuna, drained

2 tablespoons sun-dried tomatoes, chopped

1 and ½ tablespoon basil pesto

2 tablespoons black olives, pitted and chopped

Salt and black pepper to the taste

2 teaspoons pine nuts, toasted and chopped

1 tablespoon basil, chopped

Directions:

In a bowl, combine the tuna with the sun-dried tomatoes and the rest of the ingredients except the avocado and stir.

Stuff the avocado halves with the tuna mix and serve as an appetizer.

Nutrition: calories 233, fat 9, fiber 3.5, carbs 11.4, protein 5.6

Wrapped Plums

Preparation time: 5 minutes

Cooking time: 0 minutes

Servings: 8

Ingredients:

2 ounces prosciutto, cut into 16 pieces

4 plums, quartered

1 tablespoon chives, chopped

A pinch of red pepper flakes, crushed

Directions:

Wrap each plum quarter in a prosciutto slice, arrange them all on a platter, sprinkle the chives and pepper flakes all over and serve.

Nutrition: calories 30, fat 1, fiber 0, carbs 4, protein 2

Cucumber Sandwich Bites

Preparation time: 5 minutes

Cooking time: 0 minutes

Servings: 12

Ingredients:

1 cucumber, sliced

8 slices whole wheat bread

2 tablespoons cream cheese, soft

1 tablespoon chives, chopped

¼ cup avocado, peeled, pitted and mashed

1 teaspoon mustard

Salt and black pepper to the taste

Directions:

Spread the mashed avocado on each bread slice, also spread the rest of the ingredients except the cucumber slices.

Divide the cucumber slices on the bread slices, cut each slice in thirds, arrange on a platter and serve as an appetizer.

Nutrition: calories 187, fat 12.4, fiber 2.1, carbs 4.5, protein 8.2

Cucumber Rolls

Preparation time: 5 minutes

Cooking time: 0 minutes

Servings: 6

Ingredients:

1 big cucumber, sliced lengthwise

1 tablespoon parsley, chopped

8 ounces canned tuna, drained and mashed

Salt and black pepper to the taste

1 teaspoon lime juice

Directions:

Arrange cucumber slices on a working surface, divide the rest of the ingredients, and roll.

Arrange all the rolls on a platter and serve as an appetizer.

Nutrition: calories 200, fat 6, fiber 3.4, carbs 7.6, protein 3.5

Olives and Cheese Stuffed Tomatoes

Preparation time: 10 minutes

Cooking time: 0 minutes

Servings: 24

Ingredients:

24 cherry tomatoes, top cut off and insides scooped out

2 tablespoons olive oil

¼ teaspoon red pepper flakes

½ cup feta cheese, crumbled

2 tablespoons black olive paste

¼ cup mint, torn

Directions:

In a bowl, mix the olives paste with the rest of the ingredients except the cherry tomatoes and whisk well.

Stuff the cherry tomatoes with this mix, arrange them all on a platter and serve as an appetizer.

Nutrition: calories 136, fat 8.6, fiber 4.8, carbs 5.6, protein 5.1

Tomato Salsa

Preparation time: 5 minutes

Cooking time: 0 minutes

Servings: 6

Ingredients:

1 garlic clove, minced

4 tablespoons olive oil

5 tomatoes, cubed

1 tablespoon balsamic vinegar

¼ cup basil, chopped

1 tablespoon parsley, chopped

1 tablespoon chives, chopped

Salt and black pepper to the taste

Pita chips for serving

Directions:

In a bowl, mix the tomatoes with the garlic and the rest of the ingredients except the pita chips, stir, divide into small cups and serve with the pita chips on the side.

Nutrition: calories 160, fat 13.7, fiber 5.5, carbs 10.1, protein 2.2

Chapter 15. Dessert Recipes

Blueberries Stew

Preparation Time: 10 minutes

Cooking Time: 10 minutes

Servings: 4

Ingredients:

2 cups blueberries

3 tablespoons stevia

1 and ½ cups pure apple juice

1 teaspoon vanilla extract

Directions:

In a pan, combine the blueberries with stevia and the other ingredients, bring to a simmer and cook over medium-low heat for 10 minutes.

Divide into cups and serve cold.

Nutrition:

Calories 192

Fat 5.4

Fiber 3.4

Carbs 9.4 Protein 4.5

Mandarin Cream

Preparation Time: 20 minutes

Cooking Time: 0 minutes

Servings: 8

Ingredients:

2 mandarins, peeled and cut into segments

Juice of 2 mandarins

2 tablespoons stevia

4 eggs, whisked

¾ cup stevia

¾ cup almonds, ground

Directions:

In a blender, combine the mandarins with the mandarins juice and the other ingredients, whisk well, divide into cups and keep in the fridge for 20 minutes before serving.

Nutrition:

Calories 106

Fat 3.4

Fiber 0

Carbs 2.4 Protein 4

Creamy Mint Strawberry Mix

Preparation Time: 10 minutes

Cooking Time: 30 minutes

Servings: 6

Ingredients:

Cooking spray

¼ cup stevia

1 and ½ cup almond flour

1 teaspoon baking powder

1 cup almond milk

1 egg, whisked

2 cups strawberries, sliced

1 tablespoon mint, chopped   - 1 teaspoon lime zest, grated

½ cup whipping cream

Directions: In a bowl, combine the almond with the strawberries, mint and the other ingredients except the cooking spray and whisk well. Grease 6 ramekins with the cooking spray, pour the strawberry mix inside, introduce in the oven and bake at 350 degrees F for 30 minutes. Cool down and serve.

Nutrition: Calories 200 Fat 6.3 Fiber 2 Carbs 6.5 Protein 8

Vanilla Cake

Preparation Time: 10 minutes

Cooking Time: 25 minutes

Servings: 10

Ingredients:

3 cups almond flour

3 teaspoons baking powder

1 cup olive oil

1 and ½ cup almond milk

1 and 2/3 cup stevia

2 cups water

1 tablespoon lime juice

2 teaspoons vanilla extract

Cooking spray

Directions: In a bowl, mix the almond flour with the baking powder, the oil and the rest of the ingredients except the cooking spray and whisk well. Pour the mix into a cake pan greased with the cooking spray, introduce in the oven and bake at 370 degrees F for 25 minutes. Leave the cake to cool down, cut and serve!

Nutrition: Calories 200 Fat 7.6 Fiber 2.5 Carbs 5.5 Protein 4.5

Pumpkin Cream

Preparation Time: 5 minutes

Cooking Time: 5 minutes

Servings: 2

Ingredients:

2 cups canned pumpkin flesh

2 tablespoons stevia

1 teaspoon vanilla extract

2 tablespoons water

A pinch of pumpkin spice

Directions:

In a pan, combine the pumpkin flesh with the other ingredients, simmer for 5 minutes, divide into cups and serve cold.

Nutrition:

Calories 192

Fat 3.4

Fiber 4.5

Carbs 7.6

Protein 3.5

Chia and Berries Smoothie Bowl

Preparation Time: 5 minutes

Cooking Time: 0 minutes

Servings: 2

Ingredients:

1 and ½ cup almond milk

1 cup blackberries

¼ cup strawberries, chopped

1 and ½ tablespoons chia seeds

1 teaspoon cinnamon powder

Directions:

In a blender, combine the blackberries with the strawberries and the rest of the ingredients, pulse well, divide into small bowls and serve cold.

Nutrition:

Calories 182

Fat 3.4

Fiber 3.4

Carbs 8.4

Protein 3

Minty Coconut Cream

Preparation Time: 4 minutes

Cooking Time: 0 minutes

Servings: 2

Ingredients:

1 banana, peeled

2 cups coconut flesh, shredded

3 tablespoons mint, chopped

1 and ½ cups coconut water

2 tablespoons stevia

½ avocado, pitted and peeled

Directions:

In a blender, combine the coconut with the banana and the rest of the ingredients, pulse well, divide into cups and serve cold.

Nutrition:

Calories 193

Fat 5.4

Fiber 3.4

Carbs 7.6 Protein 3

Watermelon Cream

Preparation Time: 15 minutes

Cooking Time: 0 minutes

Servings: 2

Ingredients:

1 pound watermelon, peeled and chopped

1 teaspoon vanilla extract

1 cup heavy cream

1 teaspoon lime juice

2 tablespoons stevia

Directions:

In a blender, combine the watermelon with the cream and the rest of the ingredients, pulse well, divide into cups and keep in the fridge for 15 minutes before serving.

Nutrition:

Calories 122

Fat 5.7

Fiber 3.2

Carbs 5.3

Protein 0.4

Grapes Stew

Preparation Time: 10 minutes

Cooking Time: 10 minutes

Servings: 4

Ingredients:

2/3 cup stevia

1 tablespoon olive oil

1/3 cup coconut water

1 teaspoon vanilla extract

1 teaspoon lemon zest, grated

2 cup red grapes, halved

Directions:

Heat up a pan with the water over medium heat, add the oil, stevia and the rest of the ingredients, toss, simmer for 10 minutes, divide into cups and serve.

Nutrition:

Calories 122

Fat 3.7

Fiber 1.2

Carbs 2.3 Protein 0.4

Cocoa Sweet Cherry Cream

Preparation Time: 2 hours

Cooking Time: 0 minutes

Servings: 4

Ingredients:

½ cup cocoa powder

¾ cup red cherry jam

¼ cup stevia

2 cups water

1 pound cherries, pitted and halved

Directions:

In a blender, mix the cherries with the water and the rest of the ingredients, pulse well, divide into cups and keep in the fridge for 2 hours before serving.

Nutrition:

Calories 162

Fat 3.4

Fiber 2.4

Carbs 5

Loukoumade (Fried Honey Balls)

Preparation Time: 20 minutes

Cooking Time: 45 minutes

Servings: 10

Ingredients:

2 cups of sugar

1 cup of water

1 cup honey

1 ½ cups tepid water

1 tbsp. brown sugar

¼ cup of vegetable oil

1 tbsp. active dry yeast

1 ½ cups all-purpose flour, 1 cup cornstarch, ½ tsp salt

Vegetable oil for frying

1 ½ cups chopped walnuts

¼ cup ground cinnamon

Directions:

Boil the sugar and water on medium heat. Add honey after 10 minutes. cool and set aside.

Mix the tepid water, oil, brown sugar,' and yeast in a large bowl. Allow it to sit for 10 minutes. In another bowl, mix the flour, salt, and cornstarch. With your hands mix the yeast and the flour to make a wet dough. Cover and set aside for 2 hours.

Fry in oil at 350°F. Use your palm to measure the sizes of the dough as they are dropped in the frying pan. Fry each batch for about 3-4 minutes.

Immediately the loukoumades are done frying, drop them in the prepared syrup.

Serve with cinnamon and walnuts.

Nutrition: Calories: 355kcal Carbs: 64g Fat: 7g Protein: 6g

Crème Caramel

Preparation Time: 1 hour

Cooking Time: 1 hour

Servings: 12

Ingredients:

5 cups of whole milk

2 tsp vanilla extract

8 large egg yolks

4 large-sized eggs

2 cups sugar, divided

¼ cup 0f water

Directions:

Preheat the oven to 350°F

Heat the milk on medium heat until it is scalded.

Mix 1 cup of sugar and eggs in a bowl and add it to the eggs.

With a nonstick pan on high heat, boil the water and remaining sugar. Do not stir, instead whirl the pan. When the sugar forms caramel, divide it into ramekins.

Divide the egg mixture into the ramekins and place in a baking pan. Add water to the pan until it is half full. Bake for 30 minutes.

Remove the ramekins from the baking pan, cool, then refrigerate for at least 8 hours.

Serve.

Nutrition:

Calories: 110kcal

Carbs: 21g

Fat: 1g

Protein: 2g

Galaktoboureko

Preparation Time: 30 minutes

Cooking Time: 90 minutes

Servings: 12

Ingredients:

4 cups sugar, divided

1 tbsp. fresh lemon juice

1 cup of water

1 Tbsp. plus 1 ½ tsp grated lemon zest, divided into 10 cups

Room temperature whole milk

1 cup plus 2 tbsps. unsalted butter, melted and divided into 2

Tbsps. vanilla extract

7 large-sized eggs

1 cup of fine semolina

1 package phyllo, thawed and at room temperature

Directions:

Preheat oven to 350°F

Mix 2 cups of sugar, lemon juice, 1 ½ tsp of lemon zest, and water. Boil over medium heat. Set aside.

Mix the milk, 2 Tbsps. of butter, and vanilla in a pot and put on medium heat. Remove from heat when milk is scalded

Mix the eggs and semolina in a bowl, then add the mixture to the scalded milk. Put the egg-milk mixture on medium heat. Stir until it forms a custard-like material.

Brush butter on each sheet of phyllo and arrange all over the baking pan until everywhere is covered. Spread the custard on the bottom pile phyllo

Arrange the buttered phyllo all over the top of the custard until every inch is covered.

Bake for about 40 minutes. cover the top of the pie with all the prepared syrup. Serve.

Nutrition:

Calories: 393kcal

Carbs: 55g

Fat: 15g

Protein: 8g

Kourabiedes Almond Cookies

Preparation Time: 20 minutes

Cooking Time: 50 minutes

Servings: 20

Ingredients:

1 ½ cups unsalted butter, clarified, at room temperature 2 cups

Confectioners' sugar, divided

1 large egg yolk

2 tbsps. brandy

1 1/2 tsp baking powder

1 tsp vanilla extract

5/ cups all-purpose flour, sifted

1 cup roasted almonds, chopped

Directions:

Preheat the oven to 350°F

Thoroughly mix butter and ½ cup of sugar in a bowl. Add in the egg after a while. Create a brandy mixture by mixing the brandy and baking powder. Add the mixture to the egg, add vanilla, then keep beating until the ingredients are properly blended

Add flour and almonds to make a dough.

Roll the dough to form crescent shapes. You should be able to get about 40 pieces. Place the pieces on a baking sheet, then bake in the oven for 25 minutes.

Allow the cookies to cool, then coat them with the remaining confectioner's sugar.

Serve.

Nutrition:

Calories: 102kcal

Carbs: 10g

Fat: 7g

Protein: 2g

Ekmek Kataifi

Preparation Time: 30 minutes

Cooking Time: 45 minutes

Servings: 10

Ingredients:

1 cup of sugar

1 cup of water

2 (2-inch) strips lemon peel, pith removed

1 tbsp. fresh lemon juice

½ cup plus 1 tbsp. unsalted butter, melted

½ lbs. frozen kataifi pastry, thawed, at room temperature

2 ½ cups whole milk

½ tsp. ground mastiha

2 large eggs

¼ cup fine semolina

1 tsp. of cornstarch

¼ cup of sugar

½ cup sweetened coconut flakes

1 cup whipping cream

1 tsp. vanilla extract

1 tsp. powdered milk

3 tbsps. of confectioners' sugar

½ cup chopped unsalted pistachios

Directions:

Set the oven to 350°F. Grease the baking pan with 1. Tbsp of butter.

Put a pot on medium heat, then add water, sugar, lemon juice, lemon peel. Leave to boil for about 10 minutes. Reserve.

Untangle the kataifi, coat with the leftover butter, then place in the baking pan.

Mix the milk and mastiha, then place it on medium heat. Remove from heat when the milk is scalded, then cool the mixture.

Mix the eggs, cornstarch, semolina, and sugar in a bowl, stir thoroughly, then whisk the cooled milk mixture into the bowl.

Transfer the egg and milk mixture to a pot and place on heat. Wait for it to thicken like custard, then add the coconut flakes and cover it with a plastic wrap. Cool.

Spread the cooled custard-like material over the kataifi. Place in the refrigerator for at least 8 hours.

Strategically remove the kataifi from the pan with a knife. Remove it in such a way that the mold faces up.

Whip a cup of cream, add 1 tsp. vanilla, 1tsp. powdered milk, and 3 tbsps. Of sugar. Spread the mixture all over the custard, wait for it to harden, then flip and add the leftover cream mixture to the kataifi side.

Serve.

Nutrition:

Calories: 649kcal

Carbs: 37g

Fat: 52g

Protein: 11g

Revani Syrup Cake

Preparation Time: 30 minutes

Cooking Time: 3 hours

Servings: 24

Ingredients:

1 tbsp. unsalted butter

2 tbsps. all-purpose flour

1 cup ground rusk or bread crumbs

1 cup fine semolina flour

¾ cup ground toasted almonds

3 tsp baking powder

16 large eggs

2 tbsps. vanilla extract

3 cups of sugar, divided

3 cups of water

5 (2-inch) strips lemon peel, pith removed

3 tbsps. fresh lemon juice

1 oz of brandy

Directions:

Preheat the oven to 350°F. Grease the baking pan with 1 Tbsp. of butter and flour.

Mix the rusk, almonds, semolina, baking powder in a bowl.

In another bowl, mix the eggs, 1 cup of sugar, vanilla, and whisk with an electric mixer for about 5 minutes. Add the semolina mixture to the eggs and stir.

Pour the stirred batter into the greased baking pan and place in the preheated oven.

With the remaining sugar, lemon peels, and water make the syrup by boiling the mixture on medium heat. Add the lemon juice after 6 minutes, then cook for 3 minutes. Remove the lemon peels and set the syrup aside.

After the cake is done in the oven, spread the syrup over the cake.

Cut the cake as you please and serve.

Nutrition:

Calories: 348kcal

Carbs: 55g

Fat: 9g

Protein: 5g

Almonds and Oats Pudding

Preparation Time: 10 minutes

Cooking Time: 15 minutes

Servings: 4

Ingredients:

1 tablespoon lemon juice

Zest of 1 lime

1 and ½ cups almond milk

1 teaspoon almond extract

½ cup oats

2 tablespoons stevia

½ cup silver almonds, chopped

Directions:

In a pan, combine the almond milk with the lime zest and the other ingredients, whisk, bring to a simmer and cook over medium heat for 15 minutes.

Divide the mix into bowls and serve cold.

Nutrition:

Calories 174

Fat 12.1 Fiber 3.2 Carbs 3.9 Protein 4.8

Chocolate Cups

Preparation Time: 2 hours

Cooking Time: 0 minutes

Servings: 6

Ingredients:

½ cup avocado oil

1 cup, chocolate, melted

1 teaspoon matcha powder

3 tablespoons stevia

Directions:

In a bowl, mix the chocolate with the oil and the rest of the ingredients, whisk really well, divide into cups and keep in the freezer for 2 hours before serving.

Nutrition:

Calories 174

Fat 9.1

Fiber 2.2

Carbs 3.9

Protein 2.8

Mango Bowls

Preparation Time: 30 minutes

Cooking Time: 0 minutes

Servings: 4

Ingredients:

3 cups mango, cut into medium chunks

½ cup coconut water

¼ cup stevia

1 teaspoon vanilla extract

Directions:

In a blender, combine the mango with the rest of the ingredients, pulse well, divide into bowls and serve cold.

Nutrition:

Calories 122

Fat 4

Fiber 5.3

Carbs 6.6

Protein 4.5

Cocoa and Pears Cream

Preparation Time: 10 minutes

Cooking Time: 0 minutes

Servings: 4

Ingredients:

2 cups heavy creamy

1/3 cup stevia

¾ cup cocoa powder

6 ounces dark chocolate, chopped

Zest of 1 lemon

2 pears, chopped

Directions:

In a blender, combine the cream with the stevia and the rest of the ingredients, pulse well, divide into cups and serve cold.

Nutrition:

Calories 172

Fat 5.6

Fiber 3.5

Carbs 7.6 Protein 4

Pineapple Pudding

Preparation Time: 10 minutes

Cooking Time: 40minutes

Servings: 4

Ingredients:

3 cups almond flour

¼ cup olive oil

1 teaspoon vanilla extract

2 and ¼ cups stevia

3 eggs, whisked

1 and ¼ cup natural apple sauce

2 teaspoons baking powder

1 and ¼ cups almond milk - 2 cups pineapple, chopped

Cooking spray

Directions: In a bowl, combine the almond flour with the oil and the rest of the ingredients except the cooking spray and stir well.

Grease a cake pan with the cooking spray, pour the pudding mix inside, introduce in the oven and bake at 370 degrees F for 40 minutes. Serve the pudding cold.

Nutrition: Calories 223 Fat 8.1 Fiber 3.4 Carbs 7.6

CONCLUSION

As you can now see, the Mediterranean diet is not a restrictive one and it's so easy to follow.

You can eat so many wonderful and delicious dishes and you can use so many different and versatile ingredients to make them.

The Mediterranean diet will change the way you look in a matter of days. It will improve your overall health, your metabolism and it will help you lose the extra weight.

This recipes collection you've just discovered is full of delicious meals you can try at home. All these recipes taste divine and you will definitely be impressed with the textures and flavors.

So, what are you waiting for? Get your hands on a copy of this great Mediterranean diet recipes collection and make some incredible culinary feasts for all your loved ones.

Enjoy all these intense flavors and have fun discovering the Mediterranean diet!

CPSIA information can be obtained
at www.ICGtesting.com
Printed in the USA
LVHW011212200121
676908LV00030B/1180